Stories to Live By

Norman M. Pritchard

Stories to Live By
ISBN: Softcover 978-1-949888-30-0
Copyright © 2017 by Norman M. Pritchard

All rights reserved. No part of this book may be reproduced or transmitted in any form or by any means, electronic or mechanical, including photocopying, recording, or by any information storage and retrieval system, without permission in writing from the publisher.

To order additional copies of this book, contact:

Parson's Porch Books
1-423-475-7308
www.parsonsporch.com

Parson's Porch Books is an imprint of **Parson's Porch & Book Publishers** in Cleveland, Tennessee, which has double focus. We focus on the needs of creative writers who need a professional publisher to get their work to market, **&** we also focus on the needs of others by sharing our profits with those who struggle in poverty to meet their basic needs of food, clothing, shelter and safety.

To Joan, with my gratitude for love, encouragement, support and for making me think again on many occasions.

Contents

Preface 9

Ancient Stories

Abraham—One Small Step 13
   Genesis 12:1-4; John 4:46-54

Abraham and Prayer for the Nation 18
   Genesis 18:17-33; 1 Timothy 2:1-6

Jacob and His Prayers 25
   Genesis 32: 1-12

Jacob - What Goes Around Comes Around 31
   Genesis 29:15-28

Joseph and His Dreams 37
   Genesis 37:1-11

Joseph and God's Providence 43
   Genesis 50:15-21

Family Stories

Jesus' Family (1)Tamar: Family Troubles 49
   Genesis 38:12-17

Jesus' Family (2)Rahab: The Walls Come Tumbling Down ... 55
   Joshua 2:1-14

Jesus' Family (3) Ruth: 62
   Ruth 1:11-18; 4:13-17

Jesus' Family (4) Bathsheba: A Crazy Love 67
   2 Samuel 11:1-11; 12:24-25

Stories Jesus Told

Forgiveness 73
   Matt.6:12, 14-15

Take Some Humble Pie with Your Fatted Calf 79
   Luke 15:11-32

Risky Business 85
   Matthew 25:14-30

Whatever 91
   Luke 10:25-37

It's My Party 97
   Luke 15:1-3, 11b-32

Our Undiscriminating God 102
   Luke 16:1-13

Our Discriminating God 108
   Luke 16:19-31

Stories Featuring Jesus

They Watched Him 114
   Mark 3:1-6

Unreasonable Faith 120
   Mark 2:1-12

Risen Indeed 127
   Acts 9:1-20

This Life and the Next 132
   Luke 20:27-38

Stories for Jesus' Followers

A Christian to Admire 139
   John 1:35-42

An Anatomy of Ministry 144

For an ordination 144
   Luke 3:1-9, 15-17

A Procession of Thoughts 149
   Psalm 118:15-29

Remember What Your Mother Told You 156
   Acts 16:16-30

An Almost Unsung Hero 162
   Philippians 2:19-30

The Dove—Our Assurance 170
   Genesis 8:6-22

The Trouble with Nature 177
   Psalm 29

Beyond the Harold Meeker Syndrome 183
   1 Cor 12:12-31a

Light in the Darkness 190
   Isaiah 9:2-4

It Is About Me! 193

Preface

In offering these sermons to a wider readership, I am seeking to repay a debt. It is a large debt, because in many ways my Christian life has been shaped and enriched by sermons, beginning with the sermons I heard in the church in Glasgow where I grew up and where Dr Harry Thompson made scripture vividly alive. My indebtedness continues through the numerous occasions when I have been ministered to by the sermons of others, including published sermons—as many of my footnotes will demonstrate.

It was in that church in Glasgow that I heard God's call to ministry. Our pastor gave the youth group amazing freedom in all our program activities—there was, of course, no youth pastor to shepherd us. One aspect of that freedom was that each year we were invited to conduct an evening service, sermon included, and the pastor left us entirely to do it ourselves. One year, it fell to me to deliver the message. As it happened, I was in the middle of a crossroads: my plans for my future career were in doubt and ministry had unexpectedly suggested itself to me. I was resisting, feeling properly inadequate and unworthy—until that evening service. Not that my inadequacy or unworthiness had been removed, but my hesitation about pursuing this sense of call was removed and I glimpsed something of the privilege and joy that preaching offered.

I trained for the ministry of the Church of Scotland at the University of Glasgow and was blessed to be able to study for five years under Professor William Barclay and see the way he used his profound knowledge of the New Testament world to make scripture come alive and confront us with its truths. That training in the Church of Scotland introduced me to many of the fine preachers that that tradition has produced across the years, and some of their published works still occupy an honored place on my shelves. Among them is a little book on prayer by Arthur John Gossip, (wonderful name for a preacher!) *In the Secret Place of the Most High*. In it, he comments on the worship service.

> Consider the tremendous conception of the sermon in the Reformed service. The preacher has come out from the

> hush and secret of the Presence, where for a week he has been listening and brooding, face-to-face with God in a silence other [people] cannot attain, and where the divine voice can carry clearly. And now he is speaking to us in God's name, and standing in Christ's stead, bringing a message straight from the very God to very us, which, partly at least, we can really catch through the stumbling and stuttering of the man seeking to express and share it with us. That is the meaning of the ministry: why [people] are set apart. That is the purpose of the service. God is here; is taking action upon our behalf; has come with grace for us. Down on your face, and worship![1]

I read those words regularly to remind me of the seriousness of the calling to preach, and reflect on the way they affirm what a privilege preaching is.

Upon graduation, I have been called to serve congregations in Edinburgh and Ayrshire, in Scotland, in Melbourne, Australia and Bloomfield Hills in Michigan. Even after I retired, an invitation to continue in ministry offered itself and brought me to a marvelous new congregation, Christ Church of Longboat Key, FL. In all of these vastly different settings, I have been humbled by the power of scripture to speak to us, sometimes with comfort, sometimes with challenge, and I have been blessed by generously receptive, careful and caring hearers whose presence week by week implicitly asked the scriptural question, Is there any word from the Lord?[2]

Which brings me to a second dimension of the privilege that blesses the preacher. Gossip spoke of the preacher "bringing a message straight from the very God to very us" and there have been times when I have experienced that truth. One example arose from the fact that I am almost invariably accompanied by a manuscript in the pulpit, from which I may occasionally stray a little. The risk, of course, is that the preacher may lose her place. Faced with that dilemma, the preacher has two main choices: stop and try to recover the thread of the sermon, and risk embarrassing both preacher and

---

[1] A J Gossip, *In the Secret Place of the Most High*. London: Independent Press, n.d., 122.
[2] Jeremiah 37:17.

congregation, or continue speaking in a kind of ad lib improvisation on the sermon's theme. On one occasion I lost my place and opted for the later strategy. After service, one member of the congregation stayed to thank me for a sermon which spoke to her, she said, as though I knew exactly what was happening in her life at that moment. Gratified but puzzled by my failure to recognize the part of the sermon that she said had helped her, I checked my manuscript when I returned to my study. I came to realize that the help had come, not from my carefully written script, but from my panicked improvisation as I scrambled to recover my train of thought and return to the script I had prepared.

It was an experience that convinced me of the wisdom of whichever preacher it was who advised us to prepare as though there is no Holy Spirit, then preach in the conviction that there is. I think that captures the essence of preaching in a way that should make the preacher very conscious of the privilege and the challenge that preaching calls us to! When I studied preaching under Ian Pitt-Watson at Fuller Theological Seminary, I heard several variations on the words he wrote in his *Primer for Preachers:*

> I love with my whole heart this fearsome, frustrating, burdensome, exhilarating, beautiful thing we face Sunday by Sunday as we mount the pulpit steps[3]

To which I can only add, with grateful heart, Amen!

---

[3] Ian Pitt-Watson, *Primer for Preachers*. Grand Rapids, MI: Baker Book House, 1986, 16.

Abraham—One Small Step
Genesis 12:1-4; John 4:46-54

Now the LORD said to Abram, "Go from your country and your kindred and your father's house to the land that I will show you. I will make of you a great nation, and I will bless you, and make your name great, so that you will be a blessing. I will bless those who bless you, and the one who curses you I will curse; and in you all the families of the earth shall be blessed."

So Abram went, as the LORD had told him; and Lot went with him. Abram was seventy-five years old when he departed from Haran

Also, John 4:46-54

Then he came again to Cana in Galilee where he had changed the water into wine. Now there was a royal official whose son lay ill in Capernaum. When he heard that Jesus had come from Judea to Galilee, he went and begged him to come down and heal his son, for he was at the point of death. Then Jesus said to him, "Unless you see signs and wonders you will not believe." The official said to him, "Sir, come down before my little boy dies." Jesus said to him, "Go; your son will live." The man believed the word that Jesus spoke to him and started on his way. As he was going down, his slaves met him and told him that his child was alive. So he asked them the hour when he began to recover, and they said to him, "Yesterday at one in the afternoon the fever left him." The father realized that this was the hour when Jesus had said to him, "Your son will live." So he himself believed, along with his whole household. Now this was the second sign that Jesus did after coming from Judea to Galilee.

Genesis 12:4 So Abraham went, as the Lord had told him …

I have two questions for you. The first is, Are you happy with your life—or are there things you'd like to change?

I ask this question because it seems there are plenty of people around these days anxious to help you with some "life-changing" plan. I encounter them every time I start my computer. Articles pop up with titles like

- 10 happiness strategies that will change your life.

- The life-changing food you probably don't know about.
- 5 workout tricks that will change your life.

The list could go on and on … confirming the assumption that people are dissatisfied with their lot and long for a change.

The second question I have arises from that. Have you ever considered that faith could have the potential to change your life?

Many years ago, the Penguin Publishing Group was planning its series of paperbacks called 'The Penguin Classics' series. They commissioned E V Rieu to do a modern translation of the Four Gospels[4]. His son made the observation,

> It will be interesting to see what my father makes of the Gospels. It will be more interesting to see what the Gospels make of my father!

Now there's a thought! Here is a man who thinks the scriptures might just change his father! How about you? Have you ever thought, what would happen if God suddenly became real for us? For you? For me? Let me offer an answer and then explain it.

If God suddenly became real for us, I believe our lives would change. They'd become brighter, richer, fuller, more effective, more wonderful—in the sense of more full of wonder—more fulfilling and more fulfilled. We'd be twice the people we were previously! How do I know?

Look at our scripture reading today. Look at old Abraham, 75 and still going strong, but about to change: to get stronger as God calls him to a pilgrimage, to leave everything he knows and is familiar with and follow where God leads. That's some change; and, for sure, there's risk and sacrifice involved: he gives up the security of home, and the comfort of familiar routines.

---

[4] E.V. Rieu *The Four Gospels: A New Translation from the Greek*. Harmsworth: Penguin Books; Fifth impression, 1961.

But God is not calling him to deprivation and want. Listen again to the promises God makes:

> I will give you land (a home) I will make of you a great nation, and I will bless you and make your name great, so that you may be a blessing …and in you all the families of the earth shall be blessed. (vv. 2-3)

And before we imagine that this might be the first text for the prosperity gospel, "God wants me to be rich," we need to read the text properly, and see that it isn't. The blessings Abraham is promised are for him, to be sure, but for him so that through him the blessing might ripple wider and reach further and last longer. Through him a nation is born—a work of many generations—and through the nation, the world is blessed. The range of God's plan is so much longer and wider than our self-absorption can at times comprehend.

Look at the text. God makes those promises, and then Genesis adds simply, 'So Abraham went, as the Lord had told him …' It all begins with one small step…

Same thing in the New Testament when Jesus called disciples. He calls his first disciples to follow, and points to the wide horizon and the long term: Fishermen, follow me, he says, and I will make you fish for people. "And immediately they left their nets and followed him," Mark records.

And two thousand years later, the power of the impact God made on their lives has changed the world. And it all began with one small step.

Sometimes we make the Christian faith difficult, as though we have to have the answers before we begin. All the doctrines must be understood, all the standards of Christian behavior in place, all the qualifications and requirements in order—all those things to be accomplished before we can commit or perhaps, having committed to become a Christian, all those things must be in place before we can offer for some ministry or service. That's not the way it is.

Norman M. Pritchard

It's not that those things are not important; they all of them—doctrines, standards and the rest—all have their place, but they are not prerequisites.

See it in our Gospel reading. A royal official—a Gentile likely—has heard about Jesus and comes asking for help. He comes from Capernaum to Cana, a distance of 18 miles asking for healing for his sick son. Jesus assures him that his son will live. John tells us,

> The man believed the word that Jesus spoke to him and started on his way.[5]

'Started on his way'—on a journey of 18 miles, with only the promise of Jesus to go on ... That's faith, that's trust in the promise of Jesus, and it begins with one small step.

Tom Long has a wonderful story about a congregation in a college town where the atmosphere was very academic. On one visit he spoke to a man at a church pot luck supper. The man, Tom discovered, had been attending the church for ages.

> "In fact," he said, "I'm the last non-intellectual left in this congregation... I have not understood a sermon that has been preached here in twenty-five years."

So why did he stay? The man went on to say he'd never leave that church. Every Monday evening a small group of church members go to a local youth correctional facility. They play table tennis. They do Bible study. "Mainly we just get to know them and try to show them we care." Then he went on,

> I started doing this because I thought it's the sort of thing a Christian ought to do. But now, I would not miss a Monday night because I have found that it nourishes my soul... You know, you can't prove any of the promises of God in advance. But I have found that if you live them, they're true. Every one.[6]

---

[5] John 4:50.
[6] Thomas G Long, "Of This Gospel" in Svennungsen and Wiginton, *Awakened to a Calling: Reflections on the Vocation of Ministry*. Nashville: Abington, 2005, 42.

And it all begins with one small step.

You know of course that I got that phrase on the moon. "One small step" were among the first words Neil Armstrong spoke when he got out of the lunar module and stepped onto the moon's surface.

It was one small step for him, but behind it lay years of background planning, preparation and support that made it possible. Faith's just the same: there's background planning, preparation and support—we call it God's grace—and it's all been done for us. The major part of that preparation we celebrate at this table: the cross—the eternal love of God reaching into a lost and broken world and waiting for our response.

And it all begins with one small step.

Let us pray

Eternal God, as you say 'Yes' to us in Abraham and in Christ, grant us faith to say 'Yes' to you in faithful, Christian living; through Jesus Christ our Lord, Amen.

Abraham and Prayer for the Nation
Genesis 18:17-33; 1 Timothy 2:1-6

Independence Day, 2015, just after the atrocity at Charleston, VA.

The LORD said, "Shall I hide from Abraham what I am about to do, seeing that Abraham shall become a great and mighty nation, and all the nations of the earth shall be blessed in him? No, for I have chosen him, that he may charge his children and his household after him to keep the way of the LORD by doing righteousness and justice; so that the LORD may bring about for Abraham what he has promised him." Then the LORD said, "How great is the outcry against Sodom and Gomorrah and how very grave their sin! I must go down and see whether they have done altogether according to the outcry that has come to me; and if not, I will know." So the men turned from there, and went toward Sodom, while Abraham remained standing before the LORD.

Then Abraham came near and said, "Will you indeed sweep away the righteous with the wicked? Suppose there are fifty righteous within the city; will you then sweep away the place and not forgive it for the fifty righteous who are in it? Far be it from you to do such a thing, to slay the righteous with the wicked, so that the righteous fare as the wicked! Far be that from you! Shall not the Judge of all the earth do what is just?" And the LORD said, "If I find at Sodom fifty righteous in the city, I will forgive the whole place for their sake." Abraham answered, "Let me take it upon myself to speak to the Lord, I who am but dust and ashes. Suppose five of the fifty righteous are lacking? Will you destroy the whole city for lack of five?" And he said, "I will not destroy it if I find forty-five there." Again, he spoke to him, "Suppose forty are found there." He answered, "For the sake of forty I will not do it." Then he said, "Oh do not let the Lord be angry if I speak. Suppose thirty are found there." He answered, "I will not do it, if I find thirty there." He said, "Let me take it upon myself to speak to the Lord. Suppose twenty are found there." He answered, "For the sake of twenty I will not destroy it." Then he said, "Oh do not let the Lord be angry if I speak just once more. Suppose ten are found there." He answered, "For the sake of ten I will not destroy it." And the LORD went his way, when he had finished speaking to Abraham; and Abraham returned to his place.

Stories to Live By

I have two worries about this year's Independence Day holiday. One is that many people will want to turn off the news, tune out the pain and confusion of the moment and enjoy the flag, the parade, a barbecue and fireworks, and forget the world outside. That would make for an empty holiday.

The other is that there will be people, concerned for the nation, who will view our present state with deep concern, grieve our current discord, and feel the problems are too big and there's nothing we can do. That would make for a depressing holiday.

I believe there is another way.

You may be one of the 65% of all Americans, or one of the 82% of all Republicans, or one of 50% of all Democrats, who believe that the country is on the wrong track and headed in the wrong direction. If so, there is something that you can do about it. Pray for the country. Pray regularly, pray seriously, pray believingly for our country. We have a God who hears and answers prayer.

That is the meaning that shines from our scripture readings today.

That may not seem immediately obvious from our Abraham reading, because it's such a problem story, but the problems are too big for a sermon, and would take us too far from what's on our mind today.

I simply want to note that big and threatening and nasty as Sodom and Gomorrah were, Abraham prayed for them. In scripture Sodom became shorthand for wickedness—in some places sexual wickedness, in Isaiah it was political corruption, in Ezekiel it was extravagant and insolent wealth. "In fact," one commentator says, "whatever you thought was the worst wickedness, you attributed to Sodom."[7] And Abraham prayed for Sodom.

Abraham had said his personal prayers—for Sarah, to have a child; for Ishmael, the son of an irregular union, but nonetheless dear to Abraham's heart. Abraham will go on to pray for Isaac when he comes. Abraham has said his personal prayers, just as we do. Now

---

[7] Eric Routley, *Saul Among the Prophets*. London: Epworth Press, 1971, 18.

he teaches us to raise the vision of our prayers higher and broaden our petitions.

Sodom and Gomorrah represented the worst people could think of—And Abraham prayed for them.

In the New Testament, too, we find similar encouragement. Our reading from 1 Timothy today says we are to pray for everyone, including those in authority. What's remarkable here is, of course, the fact that the apostle intends prayer for the Roman Emperor, too! The powerful, pagan, soon-to-be-persecuting Roman emperor! He too needs prayer! And if that's not remarkable enough for you, remember that Jesus also told us to pray for our enemies[8]!!

So, we are to pray for our President; for our congress; for our state and local governments, as part of our praying for all God's children. How often do we do that?

I don't mean that as a rhetorical question. During my ministry in my last church, I made a suggestion during some upheaval in our national political life—I can't now remember what it was. I pointed out the burden of political office. I know there's another side, but there is also the relentless invasion of privacy, the corroding pressures on home and family life, the countless people demanding to be heard, and so on. And I said that these days, we should be grateful that anyone is willing to offer for political service.

Scripture tells us to pray for our leaders, so I made a suggestion. "After you've prayed for them, write and tell them that you have prayed and will pray for them. They need encouragement." And since, in most sermons, I'm preaching to myself at least as much as I am to the congregation, I wrote to our congressman and senators. Some time later I got a voicemail message from a senator's office. Bubbling enthusiasm, almost exuberant thanks; what a wonderful letter to receive: the senator is deeply grateful, all of us in his office are ... etc etc.

I came to the sad realization that mine was the only such letter they'd received! No one in my congregation, it seemed, had acted on my

---

[8] Matthew 5:43-48.

suggestion! Don't we care about our politicians? Don't we want to encourage them to give of their best? Or do we only want them when we think they can give us something …? Or is the problem that we don't believe in prayer? Oh, prayer is fine when we're praying for ourselves and our needs—or wants!!—but surely there's more to prayer than that.

I believe the one thing our nation needs at this present moment is prayer, the same kind of serious, wrestling, humble, honest prayer we see Abraham engage in.

Think of the resources prayer offers us, in the wake of the Charleston murders and the unrest that followed. Prayer begins in humility and offers us room for and need for confession. Listen to Presbyterian pastor John Ortberg reflecting on Charleston:

> The expressions of forgiveness from the members of that church, from parents in mind-numbing agony, are staggering to me. Jesus is in those words, for sure. Yet before I celebrate those expressions too quickly, maybe I need to listen, lest I just want to think their forgiveness resolves things. Lest I turn them into beings who have a capacity for infinite suffering that is either super-human or sub-human and means that I don't have to concern myself with their humanity.[9]

And concerning oneself about our country should lead us to reflection on the way self-assertion has become an epidemic in our day.

Love of self leads people to photograph themselves— 'selfies'—and instantly load them on to internet sites, seeking their 15 minutes of fame—every 15 minutes, every day. Major speakers have lecture invitations at universities cancelled because some students won't

---

[9] John Ortberg, The Almost Alternate Ending in Charleston *Leadership Journal* Blog June 23, 2015
http://www.christianitytoday.com/le/2015/june-web-exclusives/almost-alternate-ending-at-emanuel
ame.html?utm_source=gallireport&utm_medium=Newsletter&utm_term=13345900&utm_content=364584640&utm_campaign=2013&start=2

tolerate a viewpoint they don't like. School reading lists carry 'trigger warnings' in case a student's sense of self is violated by something they might read. How much love of self led the downfall of any of the 'personalities' involved in all those public melt-downs our culture keeps throwing up?

The story of the American revolution makes unsettling reading today. The discipline, the dedication, the sacrifices produced by ordinary people who loved their country offer a sharp contrast to the values that dominate in today's culture.

Remember Nathan Hale, the patriot hanged by the British in 1776 at the age of 21. His words have become famous: "I only regret that I have but one life to lose for my country." These days, it seems, we're not prepared to give up anything for our country, or for anyone other than the self! We need to pray for divine disinfectant to heal us of that disease!!

The Charleston horror cruelly demonstrates how love of self can quickly be corrupted into hatred of the other, especially the other who is different from me. That is in full view. The alleged shooter's desire for self-affirmation was inflamed by fear—or hatred—of others who are different, and so our latest national tragedy.

Am I right in thinking that the fear of the other who is different from us, is on the increase today?

There are those who try to foment that fear to their own advantage. Ethnic minorities are particularly vulnerable, precisely because they are different. It used to be Jews, or Italians, or Chinese, or Japanese, and, to our shame perhaps always, African Americans. These days Muslims are also vulnerable to scaremongering. We should be grateful when Christians express their faith by resisting fear and standing up to fear-mongering.

On May 29 this year, when a protest was organized against Islam and its adherents in Phoenix, Arizona, Adam Estle, the executive director of Evangelicals for Middle East Understanding, helped gather dozens of Christians to pray for peace and build bridges of reconciliation.

Estle and roughly 70 other Christians surrounded the Islamic Community Center there to protect it and its attendees. They prayed and sang as the protesters—many toting guns, drawings of Muhammed, and profanity-laced signs—defamed and denigrated Muslims and Muslim sympathizers.

Estle called his counter-protest the Love Your Neighbor Rally, an opportunity to express faith by protecting the vulnerable and loving the hateful. "Our aim is to create a physical barrier of protection with our bodies," the invitation for the event read, "and a spiritual barrier of protection as we pray for the safety of our neighbors and the flourishing of our city."[10]

The events of recent days and months contain much to discourage. It's easy to assume the problems are too deep and evil too strong. But Abraham's prayer shows that "the virtue and obedience of faithful persons are valued by God and have redemptive potential."[11]

And during the reaction to the horror of Charleston, Debbie Dills provides a wonderful incentive to pray for our nation. She's a florist who attends a small Baptist church in rural North Carolina. The day after the shooting, she was running late for work but using her drive time to pray for the families grieving the atrocity when she saw the South Carolina plate on the car in front of her.

She recognized the haircut of the man depicted as the suspect in police photographs. So she called her boss, then called the police and tailed the car until the police roadblock, set up in response to her information, enabled an arrest.

Downplaying media hype that she is a hero, she offered an alternative reading of events. She said that she believes that God is at work in his world in and through the people who believe in him and who commit their lives to him. And that being so, even the

---

[10] http://fuller.edu/About/News-and-Events/Fuller-in-the-Media/2015/Courage-to-Love-Neighbors-Rises-at-Arizona-Anti-Islam-Rally/#sthash.le35SeWa.dpuf

[11] Walter Brueggemann, *Genesis: Interpretation Commentary*. Atlanta: John Knox Press, 1982, 175.

Norman M. Pritchard

seeming accidents of life—like running late for work—can be woven into a higher purpose.

Sometimes all God needs is a faithful Christian active in prayer. And more than sometimes, all we need is God and prayer that God will use us in his service.

Have a blessed holiday!

———————

Teach us, good Lord,

to serve you as you deserve;

to give and not to count the cost;

to fight and not to heed the wounds;

to toil and not to seek for rest;

to labor and not to ask for any reward,

save that of knowing that we do your will;

through Jesus Christ our Lord. Amen.

Jacob and His Prayers
Genesis 32: 1-12

Jacob went on his way and the angels of God met him; and when Jacob saw them he said, "This is God's camp!" So he called that place Mahanaim.

Jacob sent messengers before him to his brother Esau in the land of Seir, the country of Edom, instructing them, "Thus you shall say to my lord Esau: Thus says your servant Jacob, 'I have lived with Laban as an alien, and stayed until now; and I have oxen, donkeys, flocks, male and female slaves; and I have sent to tell my lord, in order that I may find favor in your sight.'" The messengers returned to Jacob, saying, "We came to your brother Esau, and he is coming to meet you, and four hundred men are with him." Then Jacob was greatly afraid and distressed; and he divided the people that were with him, and the flocks and herds and camels, into two companies, thinking, "If Esau comes to the one company and destroys it, then the company that is left will escape."

And Jacob said, "O God of my father Abraham and God of my father Isaac, O LORD who said to me, 'Return to your country and to your kindred, and I will do you good,' I am not worthy of the least of all the steadfast love and all the faithfulness that you have shown to your servant, for with only my staff I crossed this Jordan; and now I have become two companies. Deliver me, please, from the hand of my brother, from the hand of Esau, for I am afraid of him; he may come and kill us all, the mothers with the children. Yet you have said, 'I will surely do you good, and make your offspring as the sand of the sea, which cannot be counted because of their number.'"

It is sometimes true that a crisis will bring out the best in a person: she rises to new heights to meet the crisis situation. In spiritual terms, at least for a moment or two, Jacob does that here. The prayer he offers up is superb, arising out of his personal crisis and addressed to it; but at the same time so expressive of what prayer is about that it can teach all of us how to pray.

His crisis is triggered by the news that, as he returns to face the music and meet the brother he had years ago defrauded, he is told by his advance party that Esau is coming to meet him, at the head of a band of 400 men! Jacob fears the worst, and his fear drives him to prayer. And the prayer he produced in that moment of crisis is a classic, and worthy of our imitation both in the manner of his asking and in the pattern of his praying.

'O God of my father Abraham and God of my father Isaac, O Lord who said to me, 'Return to your country and your kindred and I will do you good' ... Deliver me please from the hand of my brother, for I am afraid of him; he may come and kill us all ... Yet you have said, 'I will surely do you good ...'

He begins by looking up to God (verse 9)

When Jacob prays, 'O God of my father Abraham and God of my father Isaac, O Lord who said to me, return to your country and your kindred and I will do you good' he is deliberately focusing on God and particularly on God as he has been revealed to him: God the gracious Lord, who cares for his people and calls them into covenant relationship with himself. Notice how he begins with the love of God as known in the lives of Abraham and Isaac, and as it continues to be known in his own experience of God. In other words, as he prays, Jacob focuses on God in his saving acts, God in his loving purpose. This address to God functions as an encouragement to pray.

The pattern here is similar to the one Jesus gives us in the Lord's Prayer: 'Our Father in heaven, hallowed be your name, your kingdom come ...' (Matthew chapter 6 verses 9 to 10). God is, in the teaching of Jesus, our Father, the heavenly, holy, powerful king: in praying thus to God we approach one in whom love and power and purpose are equally combined. We are encouraged, through our praying to remember that God loves and cares and has a will and purpose for our lives.

This pattern is repeated in many of the great prayers of the church, especially the collects for the day, in which God is invoked by reference to one of his attributes: 'O God who hast prepared for them that love thee such good things as pass man's understanding, pour into our hearts ...;' ' O God, the strength of them that put their trust in thee ...'; 'O Savior of the world, who by thy cross and precious blood host redeemed us, save us and ...'

This may appear simply to be a stylized or florid introduction to prayer. It is not. It is rather what Helmut Thielicke calls getting "the exact address". The authors of such prayers

> ...wanted first and foremost to seek the face of God ... and if they wanted to 'cast all their cares upon him' they didn't start until they had pinpointed the goal of their casting. For they knew that the most important part of prayer is to come into the presence of God, because we have the promise that we will be accepted and heard.[12]

So the first lesson in praying which Jacob gives us - and it is a great encouragement - is to look up to God.

Jacob looks in at himself (verse 10)

Jacob now looks at the other part of the relationship of prayer - himself. Two feelings arise, gratitude and shame. He knows that he has already been abundantly blessed: Gods help has often been a present reality even although sometimes he was not fully aware of it, or ready to acknowledge it. Modern Christians are not all that different. It frequently takes an experience of illness or hospitalization to make us realize that we usually take the blessings of health and daily routine for granted, and do not pause to be grateful.

Jacob's pattern of praying offers an antidote to that failing. If, when we pray, we look into our own life and recall our experience of God's dealings with us - in Christ and our own experience - we will realize that we are richly blessed. And when we recall times of ingratitude, or fear, or unworthiness and are moved to repentance and shame, then the blessings of forgiveness will flow into our hearts, and again we will find ourselves blessed. That was Jacob's experience: even as he prayed, 'Lord I am not worthy ...' O he was drawing close to God.

This is also, in a strange way, further incentive to pray. It may well be true that we are not worthy of the blessings we enjoy, but we are

---

[12] Helmut Thielicke, *How to Believe Again* ET H George Anderson, London: Collins, 1973, 96.

not thereby disqualified, nor are we excluded from God's love. We are still able to come to God and bring our prayers before him.

Jacob looks round at his situation (verse 11)

Jacob is in big trouble, and he knows it. He is afraid of his brother's vengeance and needs to ask for God's help to protect both himself and his family, so his prayer now becomes one of supplication and intercession: the element of asking in prayer.

This is an important part of prayer, but one which we must handle carefully because it can be misused in ways that may lead to disappointment for us and fears that God does not hear our prayer or will not answer them. Dag Hammarskjold pointed to how we might misuse petitionary prayer when he wrote: 'Your cravings as a human animal do not become a prayer just because it is God whom you ask to attend to them.'[13] There are prayers which we have no right to bring to God - selfish prayers, unworthy prayers, prayers where we seek to manipulate God to our own advantage - like the primary student who prayed, after the geography exam, 'Dear God, please let Tokyo be the capital of China, just for one week.' Only the prayers which we can bring 'in Jesus' name' (see John chapter 14 verses 13 to 14) are really proper prayers.

Even so, the range of petitions the Bible encourages us to bring to God is astonishing. The Lord's Prayer sets the pace in its central section, when our present physical needs ('daily bread') are mentioned; our spiritual need of deliverance from past sin ('forgive us our debts') is included; and our need to be preserved from evil in the future is also included ('do not bring us to the time of trial'). Our needs cover past present and future; they range from hunger to forgiveness and protection, and they are all included in this prayer, almost as if Jesus were implying that there is no need in our life which we cannot mention in God's presence. However, I used the word 'need' - not 'want' - deliberately: there is a vast difference between asking God about our needs and asking God about our wants!

---

[13] Dag Hammarskjold, *Markings*, ET London: Faber and Faber, 1964

Jacob looks forward in hope (verse 12)

Even in his crisis, Jacob has not lost sight of the lessons God and his life have taught him. He has received undeserved blessings and unexpected promises, and on that basis, even in the face of the crisis of his brother's imminent arrival with 400 men, Jacob knows that he can still have hope. He prays to God 'Yet you have said, 'I will do you good ...' The word 'yet' is significant: it expresses faith's defiance of the worries of the moment, and faith's confidence in the God of all moments. Jacob finishes his prayer, very much as the Lord's Prayer finishes, by focusing upon God and his glorious purpose. The Lord's Prayer ends, 'For the kingdom and the power and the glory are yours, now and forever ...' and even although many commentators do not regard these words as original to the teaching of Jesus, the instinct in the early church which added them after Matthew chapter 6 verse 13 was surely right. In Genesis, Jacob finishes his prayer by fastening on to God's promise to him and thereby claiming the assurance of God's love for the future outcome of his life.

There is sound spiritual wisdom in this: at the end of our praying, when the needs we have been thinking about have seemed to grow more pressing and more urgent, especially if they have been serious ones as Jacob's were, we are directed away from them and back to God. We are thereby encouraged to close our prayer, not in fretful anxiety but in serene trust in the God to whom we have been speaking. Our needs are there - but God is also there; and as we trust in him, we know we may also look to him in confidence, faith and hope.

That is surely the secret of prayer, as Jacob himself discovered: it enfolds us in the assurance of God's presence, love and power. Many Christian people have made the discovery about prayer that in the end, the reality of God is all that matters. In the nightmare of all that she endured in the war-time concentration camps, Betsie ten Boom hung on to this truth. Her dying words to her sister Corrie were, 'We must tell people what we have learned here. We must tell them that there is no pit so deep that he the is not deeper still.'

Norman M. Pritchard

From his experience at Mahanaim, Jacob would, I think, agree. His prayer strengthened him for the difficult time ahead.

What Goes Around Comes Around
Genesis 29:15-28

Then Laban said to Jacob, "Because you are my kinsman, should you therefore serve me for nothing? Tell me, what shall your wages be?" Now Laban had two daughters; the name of the elder was Leah, and the name of the younger was Rachel. Leah's eyes were lovely, and Rachel was graceful and beautiful. Jacob loved Rachel; so he said, "I will serve you seven years for your younger daughter Rachel." Laban said, "It is better that I give her to you than that I should give her to any other man; stay with me." So Jacob served seven years for Rachel, and they seemed to him but a few days because of the love he had for her. Then Jacob said to Laban, "Give me my wife that I may go in to her, for my time is completed." So Laban gathered together all the people of the place, and made a feast. But in the evening he took his daughter Leah and brought her to Jacob; and he went in to her. (Laban gave his maid Zilpah to his daughter Leah to be her maid.) When morning came, it was Leah! And Jacob said to Laban, "What is this you have done to me? Did I not serve with you for Rachel? Why then have you deceived me?" Laban said, "This is not done in our country—giving the younger before the firstborn. Complete the week of this one, and we will give you the other also in return for serving me another seven years." Jacob did so, and completed her week; then Laban gave him his daughter Rachel as a wife.

A few years ago, Justin Timberlake had a hit record and its title was the proverb, "What goes around, comes around." The song is the schadenfreude of a man who sees that the girl who left him and broke his heart has had her heart broken when her new love left her. It's as if he was telling the girl, "Honey, you had it coming. Now you know how it feels. What goes around, comes around."

Today's Scripture reading from Genesis begins in similar vein—as Jacob, who cruelly deceived his father, was himself cruelly deceived.

He had journeyed to Haran to meet up with his wider family and find a wife from within his clan. His uncle had a beautiful daughter and Jacob fell head-over-heels in love. He was willing to work for seven years to win the right to marry Rachel because he wanted her at any cost, but also because, conveniently, it gave him an excuse to stay away from home and delay the shame of facing the family he had deceived.

But deceit ran in the family gene pool. Uncle Laban had another daughter who, it seems, had little prospect of getting married so, in a way we find hard to understand, Jacob was duped into marrying her and found, the morning after his wedding, that he had the wrong wife!

It was a cruel trick, on both Leah and Jacob, but one that Jacob richly deserved. It brought him down to earth with a thump.

When Jacob had tricked his father into giving him the blessing of the firstborn, thus disenfranchising Esau, he had been pleased, with only twinges of guilt to spoil his mood. Then, running to escape his brother's revenge, he had an awesome encounter with God at Bethel and received the promise of God's blessing, he was reassured and encouraged. When he had met Rachel, and secured the promise of marrying her, he had been elated. He must have felt his life was not only charmed, but blessed: he could do no wrong.

But he had done wrong, and Jacob had to learn that while God loves us just the way we are, he loves us too much to leave us there. And the power of this story lies in the way Jacob had it coming to him, precisely in this way.

- Jacob had used the darkness of his father's blindness to deceive him, even as Laban used the darkness of the night to switch brides.

- Jacob deceived his father to usurp the right of the firstborn child; Laban deceived Jacob to affirm the right of the firstborn child.

Jacob, you had it coming. You reap what you sow. What goes around, comes around. Deal with it.

And there's the issue: deal with it. I said this story begins in a vein of what goes around comes around. It doesn't end there, because the way Jacob does deal with it opens up a new future.

It's true of Jacob as it's true for any one of us, how we deal with the stuff of life will either make or break us. Hurts and disappointments can drive us to despair or anger or resentment that can overshadow the rest of a person's life. We've all known people soured by disappointment and seething with resentment. They're bitter, angry and aggrieved. The wrong they've suffered colors everything and blots out the good things life was also offering. Whole lives can be ruined when people choose that path!

Another response is possible—to make the wrong that's been suffered into the raw material out of which to build a new and different future. It's the response we mean when we say, "When life serves you lemons, make lemonade." Easier said than done sometimes, but certainly not impossible.

During the dark days of World War II, Viktor Frankl discovered that there were those who refused to lose their humanity despite the brutality of the POW camps.

> We who lived in the concentration camps can remember the men who walked through the huts comforting others, giving away their last piece of bread. They may have been few in number, but they offer sufficient proof that everything can be taken from [us] but one thing: the last of the human freedoms - to choose one's attitude in a set of circumstances, to choose one's own way.[14]

Your hurts, your pains, the injustices you suffer can weigh you down and ruin everything.

Or, they can become the raw material out of which you mold a new tomorrow where healing happens.

I'll never forget the father whose 21-year old son lost a courageous battle with cancer. His death nearly destroyed his father, but some time after the funeral the father came to me. "Minister, if you ever have another family in a situation like this, send for me. I want to help. I can help with what we've learned."

---

[14] Victor Frankl *Man's Search for Meaning*. New York, Simon and Shuster Pocket Books,1963, 104.

We've seen it many times. After a gun atrocity, grieving parents step up to campaign for safer gun laws. That's how the Brady campaign began. Similarly, Mothers Against Drunk Driving.

Tom Long was once getting his hair cut in a town he was visiting. The conversation got around to his job and Long told his hair stylist he taught in a theological school. She began to enthuse about her wonderful church. It was a megachurch, all personality pastor and prosperity gospel. Groaning, Long thought he was condemned to both a bad haircut *and* bad theology! Nonetheless, he asked, Has God made *you* rich?

> "Oh yes. God has made me very rich."
>
> "How so?" I asked, fully expecting tales of mortgages miraculously forgiven or Lexuses magically appearing in the driveway.
>
> "God has given me a new ministry," she said, her face now radiant. "Ten hours a week I help out at a battered women's shelter. You know, I was in an abusive relationship myself, and never thought any good would come of that. But because of my experience the women in the shelter trust me and need me and listen to me when I tell them they are loved by God. When I think about that, I know that God has made me very rich, for sure."[15]

There's almost no bad experience that can't be turned to good if we have the courage and the faith to respond by refusing to succumb to defeat and despair.

That's the way Jacob chose. He negotiated another 7-year contract with Laban and got to marry Rachel a week later.

But even when married to the girl he adored, he did not abandon or neglect the wife that Laban had tricked him into having. We haven't time today to detour round the dangers of ancient polygamy, but they were plenty—pain and bitterness and tension that lived on in

---

[15] Tom Long, "Salvos in the Worship Wars" in *The Living Pulpit*, January – March 2004, 35.

later generations as the Genesis narrative does not flinch from recounting.

But Jacob stood by Leah. He chose the way of duty and responsibility and the children Leah bore to Jacob became ancestors of people like Moses and David, and therefore also, so far as his human family is concerned, Jesus.

Jacob learned integrity, a characteristic that is noble, powerful, and powerfully healing. It's the quality that puts others before self and integrity before self-interest—or self-pity. Scripture commends it. Here's Psalm 15:

> O Lord, who may abide in your tent? Who may dwell on your holy hill?
>
> [the psalm lists those who walk blamelessly, do not slander and so on. Then adds…]
>
> Those who … stand by their oath even to their own hurt …"[16]

I'm sure you are as depressed as I am at times at the quality of life today, aptly described by Fosdick as "rich in things but poor in soul." It seems nothing is untainted. Recently, *The Economist* made the World Cup finals its cover story. The headline, "Beautiful Game, Ugly Business" explored the corruption running through the sport. So sport joins the growing list of tainted politicians, business leaders, entertainers, financiers, clergy, teachers … until we feel that corruption and decay have crept into every corner of public life.

We should not be surprised. It's what happens when faith is abandoned, or is hidden in some closet and not allowed to influence behavior. So what to do? Give in and join in? Or stand up and stand out?

Remember Solzhenitsyn's resistance to the corruption of communism in Soviet Russia?

---

[16] Psalm 15:4.

Norman M. Pritchard

The party line was to be the only truth; atheism the only creed; obedience to the state's demands the only way to live. He dubbed all that "the Lie" and said,

> And the simple step of a simple courageous man is not to take part in the lie. Let the Lie come into the world, even dominate the world, but not through me."[17]

There it is: "the last of the human freedoms - to choose one's attitude …, to choose one's own way." "But not through me."

I will be true, to God and to myself.

---

[17] Aleksandr Solzhenitsyn, *One Word of Truth* The Nobel Prize Speech. London: Bodley Head, 1972, 15-16.

Joseph and His Dreams
Genesis 37:1-11

Jacob settled in the land where his father had lived as an alien, the land of Canaan. This is the story of the family of Jacob. Joseph, being seventeen years old, was shepherding the flock with his brothers; he was a helper to the sons of Bilhah and Zilpah, his father's wives; and Joseph brought a bad report of them to their father. Now Israel loved Joseph more than any other of his children, because he was the son of his old age; and he had made him a long robe with sleeves. But when his brothers saw that their father loved him more than all his brothers, they hated him, and could not speak peaceably to him.

Once Joseph had a dream, and when he told it to his brothers, they hated him even more. He said to them, "Listen to this dream that I dreamed. There we were, binding sheaves in the field. Suddenly my sheaf rose and stood upright; then your sheaves gathered around it, and bowed down to my sheaf." His brothers said to him, "Are you indeed to reign over us? Are you indeed to have dominion over us?" So they hated him even more because of his dreams and his words. He had another dream, and told it to his brothers, saying, "Look, I have had another dream: the sun, the moon, and eleven stars were bowing down to me." But when he told it to his father and to his brothers, his father rebuked him, and said to him, "What kind of dream is this that you have had? Shall we indeed come, I and your mother and your brothers, and bow to the ground before you?" So his brothers were jealous of him, but his father kept the matter in mind.

Genesis 37:6. "...listen to this dream I have had ...

Last Tuesday night I found myself in the company of several young couples and their children. The room was full of 2- and 3- year olds and, as usual when young children are present, there was a lot of noise and some intermittent crying going on. At some point our son Andrew ended up sitting on my lap.

I noticed through the loose collar on his tee shirt that his back was covered in spots that seemed to be raised, like little blisters. He was out of sorts and looked at me and said, "I think I've gotten worse." Which puzzled me, since I hadn't known he was bad.

Norman M. Pritchard

The next thing I remember was realizing that Andrew wasn't with me anymore, and I didn't know where he was. I began to worry, and then I panicked. Then I realized I was in bed and another thought took hold: "Norman, Andrew is 34, not 2. You have been dreaming."!!

So, I had a dream.

Now where that dream came from; why I should be imagining my son of 32 years ago and what, if anything, that dream tells me about my state of mind last Tuesday night, I cannot begin to imagine.

Dreams are funny things. Sometimes they reflect what's happening in our life, or what we *want to be happening* in our life. Provided they are not simply the product of something we ate, dreams may disclose what's going on in our minds.

A few days from now, the area where we live will be taken over by one of Detroit's great institutions, the *Dream Cruise*. Lovingly preserved roadsters and other classic cars will parade up and down Woodward Avenue and thousands of people will line the roadside, to watch and, in many cases to drool--I mean, dream--to dream about owning one of those beautiful machines. Or perhaps they're dreaming of the day when things were less complicated, the summers were unending, and life was good ...

There can be so much escapism in our dreams, whether we're thinking about our dream home, or even just our dream kitchen, our dream job or dream vacation--a longing for things to be different in our lives.

There was much in Joseph's life that he wished were different. His father spoiled him, spoiled him rotten, and his brothers envied and hated him as a consequence.

The poisoned atmosphere of home must have been suffocating. His longing to escape from that and be vindicated before his family is expressed in his dreams in which he sees them all bowing before him. That picture seems pure escapism from all the lonely hurt he felt.

Notice this dream: Joseph dreams of being on top, but he does not dream of *how* he makes it to the top: no dreams of hard work, discipline, sacrifice, long hours or things like that. Isn't that the telltale of escapism? But then, aren't many of our dreams like that?

A A Milne, the author of *Winnie the Pooh*, once observed that for every person who dreams of making a fortune, there are hundreds who dream of *being left* a fortune in someone's will!! Rich without the hard work—sheer, escapist fantasy, like winning the lottery or a class action law suit ... We even do it in church.

We pray for God's kingdom to come—for faith to spread, God's love to rule, ignorance and oppression to end, violence and injustice to cease. We pray for those things, but we rarely dream of our involvement in bringing about even some small advance in those directions, or of our engagement in the fight against all that denies God's love.

We're like the disciples after Easter: we say to Jesus, 'Lord is this the time when you're going to establish the Kingdom?' That is, when *you're* going to do it? We don't always appreciate the significance of Jesus' reply:

> But you will receive power when the Holy Spirit comes upon you and you shall be my witnesses ...[18]

You will do it, Jesus says, with God's help. The best-known dreamer of the 20th century made the words 'I have a dream' famous. But for Martin Luther King Jr., the dream was not a scenario where he sat on the sidelines rooting for God, but of him actively, patiently, sacrificially getting involved and doing what he believed God wanted him to do, to help make the dream a reality.

T E Lawrence—Lawrence of Arabia—once said,

> All [people] dream: but not equally. Those who dream by night in the dusty recesses of their minds wake in the morning to find that it was vanity. But the dreamers of the

---

[18] Acts 1:8.

> day are dangerous [people], for they may act their dreams with open eyes to make it possible.

Isn't that what we see in the story of Joseph. If you're looking for great vacation reading, try the story of Joseph in Genesis 37-50. All the elements of a modern thriller are present: jealousy and intrigue, betrayal and lies, some sexual seduction--only this time temptation is resisted! --reversals and opportunities, plans and their execution, success and an ending none of characters saw coming--except Joseph the dreamer and God the greatest dreamer of all!

God is the hidden player in Joseph's life. He's hardly ever mentioned in the story, but Joseph stands in the tradition of the purposes of God that began with the promise to Abraham, first for a son, then a family and then a nation. It is God's dream that the nation thus begun would be instrumental in bringing the earth to be full of the knowledge of God, as the waters cover the sea.

We get so busy with our lives, and so taken up with our plans, our agendas, our dreams, that we leave God out of the picture. We forget God has a dream called the kingdom of God in which God's will and purpose for his children come to fruition, and the life that God's children live reflects his blessing and his love.

What if you had a part to play in helping to realize God's dreams? You, just where you are, with all the gifts and possibilities your life contains, and all the reversals and setbacks, too, because Joseph shows that they are not excluded from God's working.

One of the most remarkable stories in the biography of Rick Warren, pastor of the Saddleback megachurch, comes from his time in seminary. In those days he was a student who preached revival messages in small country churches. He and a friend went to hear W A Criswell preach at the California Southern Baptist Convention. At that time Criswell pastored a church in Dallas that was the largest Baptist church in the country. Warren felt his call to ministry affirmed in Criswell's preaching, and afterwards he stood in line to shake his hand. As Warren tells it,

> ... something unexpected happened. Criswell looked at me with kind, loving eyes and said quite emphatically, 'Young man, I feel led to lay hands on you and pray for you!' He placed his hands on my head and prayed, 'Father I ask that you give this young preacher a double portion of your Spirit. May the church he pastors grow to twice the size of the Dallas church. Bless him greatly, O Lord.'[19]

Where did that prayer come from, if not a deep spiritual connection to the things of God and the desire of God to raise up servants who will advance God's kingdom?

What if God had bigger plans for you—for us—than we or you are willing to acknowledge?

But I mustn't make the pastor's mistake of thinking only of church. Church is important, but God has more in store than church—he has the world, and all the work that sustains the life of the world.

That mighty servant of God, John Stott, died recently. He was once asked how you discover God's purpose for your life. He replied,

> Here's how to determine God's will for your life: Go wherever your gifts will be exploited the most.

That may mean—

- more concentration on home and family life, more effort at grounding children in the values that last.

- It may mean honor and integrity in a difficult situation.

- It may mean more faithfulness in business,

- more effort to redeem our politics from greed and self-interest.

---

[19] Jeffery L Sheler, *Prophet of Purpose, the Life of Rick Warren*. New York: Doubleday, 2009, 77.

Norman M. Pritchard

- It may mean more dedication to the common good.

- It may mean sacrifice of more than money.

What if we were to become, by our decision and God's good grace,

> "dreamers of the day" who "act their dreams with open eyes to make it possible..."?

Lord, bless us and use us in the service of your kingdom; take us and make us what you would have us be, for Jesus' sake. Amen

Joseph and God's Providence
Genesis 50:15-21

Realizing that their father was dead, Joseph's brothers said, "What if Joseph still bears a grudge against us and pays us back in full for all the wrong that we did to him?" So they approached Joseph, saying, "Your father gave this instruction before he died, 'Say to Joseph: I beg you, forgive the crime of your brothers and the wrong they did in harming you.' Now therefore please forgive the crime of the servants of the God of your father." Joseph wept when they spoke to him. Then his brothers also wept, fell down before him, and said, "We are here as your slaves." But Joseph said to them, "Do not be afraid! Am I in the place of God? Even though you intended to do harm to me, God intended it for good, in order to preserve a numerous people, as he is doing today."

Genesis 50:20 .... God intended it for good....

Last Christmas a family was feeling guilty that grandmother would be spending the holiday alone in her new assisted living complex. After several phone calls, a grandson was finally persuaded to change his plans and spend the holiday with her, as he was the only relative living anywhere close.

So grandmother was giving him directions on how to reach her.

"You come to the front door of the apartment complex. There is a big panel at the door. With your elbow push button 14C. That's my apartment and I'll push my buzzer to unlock the main door. Come inside, the elevator is on the right. Get in, and with your elbow hit 14. When you get out, I am on the left. You can ring my doorbell with your elbow."

"Grandma, that sounds easy, but why am I hitting all these buttons with my elbow"?

"Well, you're not going to be coming empty handed, are you?"

It's not just the holidays that rouse guilt in us, is it? All sorts of things—something we've said, or done, or left undone, a diet blown, a skill abandoned, a friend forgotten—all sorts of things can get guilt going.

As Joseph's brothers knew too well. They had brought their father Jacob down to Egypt. There'd been a happy family reunion with not too many awkward questions about the past and how Joseph, once believed dead, could now be ruler of Egypt. They settled in their new surroundings, grateful to have survived the famine... Soon year followed year in humdrum routine. For 17 years.

Then Jacob dies. And suddenly the buried past re-surfaces: and guilt mounts one more assault upon the brothers' peace of mind. "What if all this forgiveness was just pretense—a guise to keep our father happy? What if, now that Jacob's dead, Joseph wants revenge ...?" So they come to Joseph, very nervous.

Joseph weeps at the power of their guilt and fear, and says,

> Even though you intended to do harm to me, God intended it for good ...

You intended—God intended: Joseph points to the providential ordering of God in human life. And what is fascinating about this is that the story is so modern. Not just in the details of dysfunctional families, seduction, betrayal, self-interest and bad economy. But also in the way the characters live their lives without any obvious intervention of God.

This is a secular story: God does not walk about intervening and issuing directions. In just over 400 verses in the story from Genesis 37-50, if God is mentioned 10 times, that is about it, and some of these are quite incidental references. God does not have a major role to play. Think how little God appears:

The brothers' jealousy was their doing, not God's.

Was God in the caravan of traders who took Joseph off to Egypt? Well, the brothers didn't see it, they were simply glad to have him off their hands, without his blood on their hands.

In Potiphar's house, perhaps? Well, Joseph got ahead through his hard work; then got imprisoned because his loyalty to God made him refuse his master's wife's seduction.

In prison, perhaps, when Joseph interpreted the prisoners' dreams? Was that God, or was that just some special gift that Joseph had?

What about Pharaoh's dream? You could argue that both the Pharaoh's dream and Joseph's plans for famine relief were obvious enough, and did not need any involvement from God.

And as for the happily-ever-after ending with the family reunion, don't forget that in time Israel fell into slavery in Egypt, and it took the Exodus to get them out again.

There's little evidence of God directly at work.

And yet, Joseph is correct: The end result is a glorious outcome wrung from an unpromising situation. God was working his purpose out. None of the characters at any time can see what God is doing, but God was there and bringing his purpose to fruition.

I like that thought. Sometimes people are so concerned to commend their faith, they paint a picture of God at work with big, bold strokes and vivid colors and an inscription all BLOCK CAPITALS and exclamation points!! Sometimes they strain for so much certainty: 'God did this.' 'God told me ...' "God does not talk all the time," Fred Craddock says.[20]

Craddock once had a tour guide in Israel tell him about a rabbi who explained everything in the bible two different ways.

> When he would come to a miracle, he would explain it two different ways, and his reason was this: If something happens and you can't explain it another way, then God didn't do it.

---

[20] Fred Craddock, *Preaching*. Nashville: Abingdon Press, 1985, 53.

> That's not bad. God does not paint you into a corner and say, 'Now, you weasel, you don't have a choice,' so that the weasel will say, 'I don't have a choice, I believe.'[21]

God's work is often hidden underneath the surface of our lives, down between the crevices of our thoughts and actions.

At no stage in Joseph's story does God pop up to say, "It's alright; these people don't mean Joseph any harm, they are acting to advance my will." The opposite is true: *they do mean harm* towards Joseph, and they act accordingly. The last thing on their mind was God, his presence or his purpose!

The betrayals, the anguish, the helplessness are not removed. At no stage could Joseph see the end result; any more than his brothers or Pharaoh.

And yet, God was present, and his purpose was being carried out.

We can see God at work in Joseph—in his loyalty to God and faithfulness to his dream; even though there were dark days when those seemed hollow indeed!

Perhaps that's all God needs. When Paul says

> We know that all things work together for good for those who love God, who are called according to his purpose. (Romans 8:28)

He's not suggesting that everyone is guaranteed a happy ending, nor is he inviting some horse trading: 'I'll love God if God will reward me.' Paul immediately defines 'those who love God' as 'those who are called according to his purpose.'

He means that those who respond to God's call can be, like Joseph, the raw material through whom God can work, agents of God's

---

[21] Edd. Mike Graves and Richard F Ward, *Craddock Stories*. St Louis: Chalice Press, 2001, 39.

good. All it takes is faith: 'Take my life and let it be consecrated, Lord, to thee.'

It's wonderfully suggestive that the origins of this church are hidden from us. We know this church was founded because Edwin George made a promise to God; we don't know why he made his promise. It may have been on a bad day, part of a 'Lord, help me' prayer. Or it may have been on a good day when he humbly realized his success was built on gifts not of his accomplishing, like all our successes. Or it may have simply been his openness to God for all the joy of living.

The hidden part is not as important now as the sight of what God can do through any one of us when we allow God to be part of our story and when we offer ourselves to God to use. Of course, whether we know it or not, God *is* part of our story: we just don't always see.

C S Lewis once imagined that when we get to heaven, we will say to God, 'So it was *you* all along. Everyone I ever loved, it was you. Everything decent or fine that ever happened to me, everything that made me reach out and try to be better, it was you all along.'[22]

That's partly why we come to church—to make room for God in our lives, to remember what the pressures of a given moment all too easily obscure, that it is only in God that 'we live and move and have our being.' We belong to church to reorient our lives to God and to the doing of God's will, so God can share our days and to use us to get his blessing out to others.

'So it was you'—the people in my life, the things to do, the pleasures, the challenges, the joys, the sorrows, the casual meetings and the deep encounters, 'So it was you.'

> We know that all things work together for good for those who love God, who are called according to his purpose.

And that great verse in Romans 8 leads to another, even greater, verse:

---

[22] Cited from Tom Long, *Testimony: Talking Ourselves into Being Christian.* San Francisco: Jossey-Bass, 2004, 126.

> For I am convinced that neither death nor life ... nor things present nor things to come, nor powers, ... nor anything else in all creation will be able to separate us from the love of God in Christ Jesus our Lord.

It is on that text that our faith is based. It is on that text that this church was built. It is on that text—and only on that text—that it will continue.

Jesus' Family (1)
Tamar: Family Troubles
Genesis 38:12-17

In course of time the wife of Judah, Shua's daughter, died; when Judah's time of mourning was over, he went up to Timnah to his sheepshearers, he and his friend Hirah the Adullamite. When Tamar was told, "Your father-in-law is going up to Timnah to shear his sheep," she put off her widow's garments, put on a veil, wrapped herself up, and sat down at the entrance to Enaim, which is on the road to Timnah. She saw that Shelah was grown up, yet she had not been given to him in marriage. When Judah saw her, he thought her to be a prostitute, for she had covered her face. He went over to her at the road side, and said, "Come, let me come in to you," for he did not know that she was his daughter-in-law. She said, "What will you give me, that you may come in to me?" He answered, "I will send you a kid from the flock." And she said, "Only if you give me a pledge, until you send it."

Matthew 1:3 ...and Judah the father of Perez and Zerah by Tamar

We all learned in writing class in school about the importance of the introduction. It lays the groundwork for everything that follows. In that case, what on earth was Matthew thinking?

Matthew begins with the family tree of Jesus, 17 verses naming the ancestors of Jesus. The list contains some well-known people, but includes others we've never heard of. Curiously, among the people we *have* heard of, are four women and those women have stories that are messy and in places murky, even immoral. So, when the Letter to the Hebrews tells us that Jesus became like us "in every respect,"[23] we can see that this included having a family with some awkward relatives, just like us.

Fred Craddock's sister loved genealogy and she was fascinated to discover an ancestor called Ruby Craddock, who had not joined the family in migrating to America.

---

[23] Hebrews 2:17.

Eventually she reported, "I found Ruby."

"Good," [Craddock] said. "What did you find out about Ruby?"

She said, "You don't want to know."

Turns out Ruby had moved to London and ran a house of ill repute! Craddock commented, "I assured my sister that this was another branch of the family and not to worry about it."[24]

I understand their embarrassment. My family name has a special niche in the history of my native city. In 1854, Dr Edward Pritchard wrote himself into the history of Glasgow by being the last man to get a public hanging in the city. And my wife is not too keen that I research the details, since he was hanged for murdering his wife and her maid!

I mean, what if he was related; what if I have some of his DNA in me ...? That's the trouble with families: traits and characteristics are passed on. I didn't read it, but I saw an article on the web last week titled "Help! My Father Is In Prison. Do I Have His DNA?"

What if Jesus had some of the ancestral DNA that ran in his family ...?

Matthew shows us that the family into which Jesus was born had as complex a family history as any family. It had its share of awkward stories and embarrassing relatives. And the women Matthew includes in the family tree of Jesus are highly embarrassing. Their stories are sensational, at times quite shocking, and today's story of Tamar is not the sort of thing we want to read to our children!

Tamar was the victim of two, probably loveless, marriages--certainly her second husband resented their relationship. Being twice widowed, therefore, might not have been too bad, except that it left her without status or security and threw her on the mercies of her father-in-law, Judah. And Judah had few mercies to offer.

---

[24] Fred Craddock, *The Cherry Log Sermons*. Louisville: Westminster John Knox Press, 2001, 2.

He ignored her; refused to acknowledge his responsibility for her. In that ancient world, that was a cruel and dangerous thing to do. It left Tamar to her own devices. Fortunately for her, she had a few. We read part of the story of how she managed to trick Judah by a desperate, immoral ploy into acknowledging her rights and treating her with the respect she deserved.

And as scripture was read, you probably thought, "This story's in the Bible...? Why didn't I didn't know that story was there ...?"

The answer is: because the story is so shocking. One of the early spiritual fathers of Israel behaved unworthily. Injustice, oppression and selective morality are not edifying, and we don't expect them in the good book. But that may be the very reason they are there.

The Bible does not pretend that all is right with the world. The Bible shows the truth of human life. It shows sin, injustice and oppression, violence and abuse, even involving people who should be bound by love and commitment. We should be grateful that our scriptures address life as it is and challenge us towards life as God intended it to be.

Tamar stands in scripture as a woman who demanded respect, who deserved to be noticed and not cast off. I think some of that DNA can be seen in Jesus. That's how he was—he wanted people to be respected, not cast off, not ignored.

One of the things that shines most clearly through the ministry of Jesus is the way—quite astonishing for his day—that he treated everyone with respect. The lost and the last and the least were priorities for him.

- Women, children, Samaritans, tax collectors, for instance.
- The man "covered in leprosy" whom Jesus healed by touching him, ignoring the risk of contamination;[25]

---

[25] Luke 5:12.

- The woman who touched the hem of his garment: "Daughter," he called her, "your faith has made you well..."[26]
- Zacchaeus, "This man too is a son of Abraham..."[27] he belongs.
- Bartimaeus—not to be ignored just because the crowd disregarded him;
- The woman who anointed his feet, the widow with her two copper coins...
- "Whatever you did to one of the least of these my brothers and sisters, you did to me."[28]

And here's a second thing to be grateful for this week: that Jesus treated us with that same respect on our journey towards faith. Our questions were dealt with, our doubts addressed and our status as God's children respected, even as God helped us to find our way home. Psalm 103:10 assures us:

> He does not deal with us according to our sins, nor repay us according to our iniquities. For as the heavens are high above the earth so great is his steadfast love toward us.

That's a memory we should always keep warm. It will nourish a spirit of gratitude and thanksgiving that will sustain us if we face days when faith falters and it will inspire us for times when faith needs to be strong. Like now.

Despite the blessings we enjoy, we are living in disturbing times. The atmosphere we breathe is thick with frustration, anger, fear and disrespect. There's been an upsurge of hate crimes.

Tim Suttle pastors a church in a suburb of Kansas City where the neighborhood is mostly Hispanic, predominantly poor, and definitely living on the margins. Suttle says,

---

[26] Mk.5:25ff.
[27] Luke 19:9
[28] Matt.25:40.

> There's a lot of pain & fear in our neighborhood right now. Members of my congregation are wondering if their lives are about to be turned upside down....

Last Wednesday, they held a church gathering. 12 of the 16 in his youth group are Hispanic, and they all turned up, with stories of harassment and abuse they'd received at school.

> One young man was called a "stupid illegal" to his face. This is a sweet kid, a good kid, who's just started to trust our church. One kid shared a text saying, "It hurts seeing people call Mexicans lazy when I see my Mom & dad come home from work tired after working two jobs that we *stole*."

Suttle shared more of the same. What to do?

> We ended with a prayer exercise. We all came to the front of the church and stood in a circle. It was a tight squeeze, so most of us were nearly touching shoulders. I handed out copies of *The Prayer of St. Francis*, and we went around the circle, each person reading one line of the prayer. When one person ended the prayer, the next person began it again. Around and around we went. We must have read it more than a dozen times together. At first people were nervous, a few people used their best TV host voice. But after a while the words began to sink in. Every once in a while, when it was their turn to read, people would have to gather themselves. Arms started to go around shoulders. I could sense the emotion, and hear the sniffles and see the tears. It was a beautiful moment.

> "Lord, make me an instrument of Your peace." ... your peace. Where there is injury, let me sow pardon. Where there is discord, let me sow harmony. Where there is doubt and despair, let me sow faith and hope.

Suttle concluded,

> I do not know if this is possible for a culture so bitterly divided. But I am certain we have to find a way to do this as

the church. Our legitimacy, our very being, depends upon it.[29]

I am grateful that those kids turned to church when faced with prejudice and abuse. I am grateful that that congregation reached for God's grace, not only as a refuge, but also as a resource: *make me an instrument of your peace.*

I am especially grateful that in a broken world, our Jesus is a healer and redeemer. We need him more than ever.

Lord, make me an instrument of your peace.
Where there is hatred, let me sow love; where there is injury, pardon; where there is discord, harmony; where there is error, truth; where there is doubt, faith; where there is despair, hope; where there is darkness, light; and where there is sadness, joy.
O Divine Master, grant that I may seek not so much to be consoled as to console;
to be understood as to understand; to be loved as to love.
For it is in giving that we receive;
it is in pardoning that we are pardoned;
and it is in dying that we are born to eternal life. Thanks be to God, Amen.

---

[29] Tim Suttle "Here's What I Told My Church After the Election." Patheos Blog, November 15, 2016
http://www.patheos.com/blogs/paperbacktheology/2016/11/heres-what-i-told-my-church-after-the-election.html

Jesus' Family (2)
Rahab: The Walls Come Tumbling Down
Joshua 2:1-14

Then Joshua son of Nun sent two men secretly from Shittim as spies, saying, "Go, view the land, especially Jericho." So they went, and entered the house of a prostitute whose name was Rahab, and spent the night there. The king of Jericho was told, "Some Israelites have come here tonight to search out the land." Then the king of Jericho sent orders to Rahab, "Bring out the men who have come to you, who entered your house, for they have come only to search out the whole land." But the woman took the two men and hid them. Then she said, "True, the men came to me, but I did not know where they came from. And when it was time to close the gate at dark, the men went out. Where the men went I do not know. Pursue them quickly, for you can overtake them." She had, however, brought them up to the roof and hidden them with the stalks of flax that she had laid out on the roof. So the men pursued them on the way to the Jordan as far as the fords. As soon as the pursuers had gone out, the gate was shut.

Before they went to sleep, she came up to them on the roof and said to the men: "I know that the LORD has given you the land, and that dread of you has fallen on us, and that all the inhabitants of the land melt in fear before you. For we have heard how the LORD dried up the water of the Red Sea before you when you came out of Egypt, and what you did to the two kings of the Amorites that were beyond the Jordan, to Sihon and Og, whom you utterly destroyed. As soon as we heard it, our hearts melted, and there was no courage left in any of us because of you. The LORD your God is indeed God in heaven above and on earth below. Now then, since I have dealt kindly with you, swear to me by the LORD that you in turn will deal kindly with my family. Give me a sign of good faith that you will spare my father and mother, my brothers and sisters, and all who belong to them, and deliver our lives from death." The men said to her, "Our life for yours! If you do not tell this business of ours, then we will deal kindly and faithfully with you when the LORD gives us the land."

Matthew 1:5 …and Salmon the father of Boaz by Rahab …

Norman M. Pritchard

When we open our Christmas cards each year, one of the phrases we see repeatedly is "peace on earth". Peace ... a sentiment as universal as it is elusive. The reality of human experience suggests that the answer to Rodney King's anguished question, "Can't we all just get along?" is, increasingly, No, we can't. Peace is elusive. Barriers are stubborn things.

One of the great poems in American literature is Robert Frost's "Mending Walls." In that poem, a New England farmer contacts his neighbor in the spring to rebuild the stone wall between their properties. As the men work, the farmer wonders why they're doing it. They're neighbors, there are no issues between them, why do they need a wall? Twice, he says, "Something there is that doesn't love a wall" but his neighbor counters twice with the proverb, "Good fences make good neighbors."[30]

We don't always want to know that if we are to have peace, we're going to have to come out from behind the walls and meet our neighbor.

Interestingly, the Letter to the Ephesians speaks about peace and locates it in Jesus. Eph.2:14 talks of Jesus and says,

> For he is our peace. In his flesh he has made [us] into one and has broken down the dividing wall, that is the hostility between us.

A dividing wall of enmity and hostility being broken down ... it reads like a description of the events of 1989, when the wall dividing East and West Germany came down, the first sign of the end of communism. It was one of the most dramatic events of recent times.

Barriers coming down; old hostilities dying and talk of reconciliation—these ideas echo the language of Advent. Words like peace, reconciliation, hope, are rich in theological significance and express part of the meaning of Christ's coming into the world.

---

[30] Robert Frost "Mending Wall" *North of Boston*. David Nutt, 1914. Accessed at http://www.english.upenn.edu/~afilreis/88/frost-mending.html
[2] Ephesians 2:14

Ephesians expresses that meaning this way: In his flesh he has made [us] into one and has broken down the dividing wall, that is the hostility between us ...[31]

In Christ, the walls come tumbling down ....

You remember the allusion in these words? Originally, when the children of Israel entered the promised land, it was the walls of Jericho which came tumbling down. In that event, the air was thick with hostility and the noise of battle, and yet 1200 years before Christ came, there was also a foretaste of his work of reconciliation, a preview of the freedom he wants to bring to human lives.

Rahab is the preview. She knew all about walls—she lived with them, literally and metaphorically. Her house was built on the city wall of Jericho. That was convenient to her work, for she worked in the fields outside the city growing flax. That work paid badly and to make ends meet, Rahab did other work. Her house on the walls of the city meant she knew when travelers came, and she could offer them hospitality—and other services. She was a prostitute, probably forced by economic needs into that work, like the millions today, many of them just children, trapped in the global sex industry—one of the great shames of the 21st century.

For Rahab, you can imagine the barriers that went up in Jericho to keep her at a distance. The walls of respectability would be built up high, to keep her securely on the outside and force her to live as one of the marginalized poor.

That's the kind of life where isolation leads to desperation and despair. I wonder if her desperation and despair made her open to helping the Israelites? That, and the fact that she saw the hand of God at work in the progress Israel was making towards Canaan.

Whatever it was, Rahab decided to take the risk of reconciliation—of helping enemies and turning them into friends. She hid Joshua's spies and gained them secure passage through the land, and in return was promised—and received—a place within Israel. When Jericho was captured, she was saved and brought into the people of God. Israel remembered her story.

Christians remember her story too. Rahab is mentioned three times in the New Testament.

- James uses her as an example of someone who put faith to work.
- She is listed among the great exemplars of faith in Hebrews 11.
- And, of course, Matthew included her in the family tree of Jesus as one of the ancestors of King David.

So the risks she took for reconciliation paid off.

Those risks she took were considerable. Her own people, for one thing, would have regarded her as a traitor, for helping the enemy. And could she trust the enemy? Her nervousness is clearly seen in her conversation with the spies and the way she asks for guarantees that they'll remember her and keep her safe when the walls of Jericho fall.

Her story reminds us that if we want peace, and hunger for reconciliation, there are risks to be taken; trust is required. And both are central to the concepts of forgiveness and reconciliation that Jesus embodied and offers.

The idea of reconciliation through Jesus is central to our faith. We need, and want and gladly receive his forgiveness that reconciles us to God. And we note how frequently Jesus worked for reconciliation and broke down walls.

It started at his birth. There was no room for them in the inn, Luke tells us. So he was born in a stable—a cave, as tradition has it, outside the walls. The pattern continued. In his ministry, he scandalized the religious people by ignoring the walls of separation and welcoming the outsiders. Samaritans; the Gerasene demoniac[32]; a Roman

---

[32] Mark 5.

centurion[33]; a Syrophoenician woman[34]; the Greeks at Passover who wanted to see him[35]; tax collectors; the people written off as "sinners." Again, and again, walls that people erected—especially religious people—came tumbling down.

But we don't always make the connection with the cost of reconciliation

It was no accident that when he died, it was "outside the city wall", so that it could clearly be seen that his death was for all, that the reconciliation and hope his love provided are not to be walled up and become the preserve of only one group, or only a few, or only the people like us, or whatever other restriction we try to apply. God so loved the world … God wants the walls to come tumbling down.

> For he is our peace… he … has broken down the dividing wall

But that gift is also our obligation. Do we always hear the obligation we repeat each time we say the Lord's Prayer? "Forgive us … as we forgive." Paul clearly understands both the gift and the obligation:

> In Christ God was reconciling the world to himself, not counting their trespasses against them, and entrusting the ministry of reconciliation to us.[36]

We are to forgive, as we are forgiven.

John Ortberg has a remarkably story that centers on the reality of reconciliation. It's the story of Mary and Oshea, who overcame a terrible past. Oshea murdered Mary's only son and was imprisoned for the crime. Good Christian that she was, Mary tried to forgive him, but found the pain would not go away. For twelve years, she could not find peace. Eventually, she overcame the resistance of the department of corrections and arranged to meet Oshea. As Ortberg tells the story,

---

[33] Luke 7:2; the Canaanite woman
[34] Mark 7:26
[35] John 12:20.
[36] 2 Corinthians 5:19.

Mary went with her friend Regina to the meeting. "It's a good thing God sends us two by two," Mary said. "When I got halfway up the ramp, I said, 'God, I cannot do this.' I would have gone home. Regina pushed me the rest of the way up the ramp."

Mary began that first conversation with Oshea with a carefully prepared thought. "I don't know you. You don't know me. Let's just start there."

The idea that she wanted to know him before judging him loosened something in his spirit. He decided he would trust the process. They talked for hours.

By the end of the first interview, Oshea asked Mary if he could hug her.

She said yes.

When his arms went around her, the floodgates burst. She sobbed. Oshea immediately had second thoughts about the hug. *I had been in prison twelve years, around hardened criminals; this was the scariest moment of my life.*

'The scariest moment' in his life because he saw the pain and the forgiveness. But the risk paid off. Oshea now lives next door to Mary; he has a job and he goes to school. He says,

Sometimes when I'm down, discouraged, when things aren't working, I look at Mary's face. And I say, "Hey, she gave me another chance. I need to give myself a chance.

Ortberg comments,

We sometimes speak of forgiveness as a tool for the victim's release from pain. And it is that. But it is more. Oshea and Mary have given each other gifts that neither would ever have known without the miracle of forgiveness.

It happened because a long time ago someone said, "Love your neighbor" and "Love your enemy." And an enemy became a neighbor. [37]

The walls came tumbling down.

For he is our peace. In his flesh he has made [us] into one and has broken down the dividing wall, that is the hostility between us.

Reconciliation. Peace. Life made new. Wonderful Christmas gifts.

---

[37] John Ortberg, *Who Is This Man?* Grand Rapids: Zondervan, 101.

Jesus Family (3) Ruth
Ruth 1:11-18; 4:13-17

But Naomi said, "Turn back, my daughters, why will you go with me? Do I still have sons in my womb that they may become your husbands? Turn back, my daughters, go your way, for I am too old to have a husband. Even if I thought there was hope for me, even if I should have a husband tonight and bear sons, would you then wait until they were grown? Would you then refrain from marrying? No, my daughters, it has been far more bitter for me than for you, because the hand of the LORD has turned against me." Then they wept aloud again. Orpah kissed her mother-in-law, but Ruth clung to her. So she said, "See, your sister-in-law has gone back to her people and to her gods; return after your sister-in-law." But Ruth said, "Do not press me to leave you or to turn back from following you! Where you go, I will go; Where you lodge, I will lodge; your people shall be my people, and your God my God. Where you die, I will die— there will I be buried. May the LORD do thus and so to me, and more as well, if even death parts me from you!" When Naomi saw that she was determined to go with her, she said no more to her....

So Boaz took Ruth and she became his wife. When they came together, the LORD made her conceive, and she bore a son. Then the women said to Naomi, "Blessed be the LORD, who has not left you this day without next-of-kin; and may his name be renowned in Israel! He shall be to you a restorer of life and a nourisher of your old age; for your daughter-in-law who loves you, who is more to you than seven sons, has borne him." Then Naomi took the child and laid him in her bosom, and became his nurse. The women of the neighborhood gave him a name, saying, "A son has been born to Naomi." They named him Obed; he became the father of Jesse, the father of David.

Matthew 1:5 ... and Boaz the father of Obed by Ruth

Dean Nelson is a journalism professor in California. He's a marvelous storyteller, as the story of his 25th wedding anniversary demonstrates.

In two years of planning for an anniversary trip to Belgium, he and his wife covered every detail: the flights, their accommodations, the grandmother to watch their kids. They even revised their wills, and

Stories to Live By

the Friday before their departure they went to an attorney to get the updated wills notarized. Their passports were their ID.

In the waiting room, Nelson flipped through his passport letting the immigration stamps remind him of some marvelous trips. I'll let Nelson take up his story.

> When I got to the front of the passport, my eyes wandered down the information lines. That's when the volume of voices in the room went silent, the walls went white, the orbit of the earth slowed to a stop, and the temperature dropped 50°.
>
> "Did you hear me?"
>
> I recognized the voice. It sounded like my wife's. She was looking at me funny.
>
> "When does your passport expire?" I could have sworn that cold air came out of her mouth, just like Bruce Willis's wife at the end of the movie *The Sixth Sense*. Suddenly I could see dead people. They all looked like me.
>
> I handed her my passport and put my head in my hands. She handed the document to the notary. No one spoke.

The attorney had an idea, but it wouldn't work in time. Changing their flights was out—too expensive.

Then, at the back of his passport Nelson noticed the telephone number of the service he had used to get entry visas for previous trips. He called. They could help. They would fax him some forms which he should sign and return to them by courier with his expired passport. Nelson complied. Looking promising! Nelson continued:

> Things seemed okay between my wife and me on the surface. We told the kids about it. My daughter would pass me in the house, pause, and hug me unsolicited, as if it were my last cigarette before the execution. I caught my son staring at me from another room. "What?" I asked. He slowly shook his head. "You are so screwed," he said.

On Monday morning Nelson called Washington. They had processed the paperwork and his passport was being rushed through the US State Department. He should have it by Tuesday, one day before departure. A little tight, but manageable.

Monday afternoon, disaster. He had omitted to sign one piece of paper and his application had been rejected. It's Monday afternoon. The flight is Wednesday morning. Again, Nelson's account:

> My wife saw my body language and stood behind the chair I was sitting in as I discussed my options on the phone. She reached down and began to massage my shoulders. I tucked my chin at first, hoping she wasn't actually feeling for my windpipe, but when I realized she was getting the picture that our anniversary trip was not going to happen because of me, after two years of planning, and she was still willing to share this shameful moment with me, I understood the concept of grace.

His visa company was not finished, however; they would fax a replacement form and if Nelson signed it and faxed it back, they would resubmit his application first thing Tuesday morning and, all going well, they might have his passport to him by 8am Wednesday. The airport shuttle was booked for 9:30am. You can imagine the tension.

> That night I woke up at 3am and turned on the television to see if there were any storms or accidents on the East Coast. I woke up again at 5 and saw that Marcia was already up, staring out the kitchen window into the darkness.
>
> At 7.30am a van pulled up in front of the house. The driver had an envelope. I signed for it before he was completely out of the vehicle. Two hours later another van arrived and took us to the airport....
>
> I remember the trip. I remember the tension I caused. But what I remember most was, at my lowest point I did not get condemnation. I got a neck rub. I got a massage that said,

"We're in this together, regardless of how badly you screwed this up."[38]

It's the second-best description of human love I know. 'Second best,' because the best occurs in our reading today, when Ruth promises Naomi:

> *Where you go, I will go;*
> *where you lodge I will lodge;*
> *your people shall be my people,*
> *and your God my God.*
> *Where you die, I shall die*
> *there be buried.*
> *I solemnly declare before the Lord,*
> *that nothing but death will part me from you.*[39]

Ruth became great-grandmother of King David, and brought her loving spirit into the family that, humanly speaking, produced the Messiah. Only that's not right, the DNA of Ruth's love first came from God and is expressed in the life and ministry of Jesus. Love as grace. Love as giving and forgiving.

- Where you go, I will go. —The incarnation: Jesus coming to earth. Christ with us in life.
- your people shall be my people. — Christ creating our faith fellowship.
- Where you die, I shall die. — Having loved his own, John's gospel tells us, he loved them to the end.[40]
- and your God will be my God. – Christ's sacrifice bringing us to God and allowing us to call God, Abba, Father, just as he did.

---

[38] Dean Nelson *God Hides in Plain Sight*. Grand Rapids, MI.: Brazos Press, 2009, 139ff.
[39] Ruth 1:16-17, *Revised English Bible*.
[40] John 13:1.

- And then, going beyond Ruth's 'nothing but death will part us' we get Paul's great truth that there is nothing in life or in death that can separate us from the love of God in Christ Jesus.[41]

The humility, the grace, the unconditional love we see in Ruth find fullest expression in the coming of Jesus to our world.

The gift of love at Christmas! Wonderful!

---

[41] Romans 8:38-39

Jesus' Family (4) Bathsheba: A Crazy Love
2 Samuel 11:1-11; 12:24-25

In the spring of the year, the time when kings go out to battle, David sent Joab with his officers and all Israel with him; they ravaged the Ammonites, and besieged Rabbah. But David remained at Jerusalem. It happened, late one afternoon, when David rose from his couch and was walking about on the roof of the king's house, that he saw from the roof a woman bathing; the woman was very beautiful. David sent someone to inquire about the woman. It was reported, "This is Bathsheba daughter of Eliam, the wife of Uriah the Hittite." So David sent messengers to get her, and she came to him, and he lay with her. (Now she was purifying herself after her period.) Then she returned to her house. The woman conceived; and she sent and told David, "I am pregnant."

So David sent word to Joab, "Send me Uriah the Hittite." And Joab sent Uriah to David. When Uriah came to him, David asked how Joab and the people fared, and how the war was going. Then David said to Uriah, "Go down to your house, and wash your feet." Uriah went out of the king's house, and there followed him a present from the king. But Uriah slept at the entrance of the king's house with all the servants of his lord, and did not go down to his house. When they told David, "Uriah did not go down to his house," David said to Uriah, "You have just come from a journey. Why did you not go down to your house?" Uriah said to David, "The ark and Israel and Judah remain in booths; and my lord Joab and the servants of my lord are camping in the open field; shall I then go to my house, to eat and to drink, and to lie with my wife? As you live, and as your soul lives, I will not do such a thing."

…. Then [after their son died] David consoled his wife Bathsheba, and went to her, and lay with her; and she bore a son, and he named him Solomon. The LORD loved him, and sent a message by the prophet Nathan; so he named him Jedidiah, because of the LORD.

Matt.1:6 Jesse was the father of King David. David was the father of Solomon (his mother had been the wife of Uriah) …

It's 53 years since President Kennedy was assassinated, and he still attracts attention. Last week, I was in the dentist's waiting room, leafing through the magazines and I came across an article in *Men's Health* on JFK and his sexual exploits.

My thinking moved from Kennedy to King David. They had a lot in common. Both were young, good looking, charismatic leaders who generated great excitement and who became very popular. Both guided nations out of uncertainty into a sense of prosperity and well-being. Both lived in up-beat atmospheres. Both created a Camelot mythology--Washington under Kennedy, and Jerusalem under David. The parallels are close.

And the parallels include the dark side both to Kennedy's and David's Camelots. In David's case, the dark side can be summed up by the name Bathsheba. The story of David and Bathsheba is the story of the greatest shame of the greatest king Israel ever had.

It is a story of lust and adultery, of deception and betrayal, of murder and treachery.

And it's a story that points to the meaning of Christmas.

I don't just mean that, later, David and Bathsheba became the parents of Solomon, through whom Matthew traces the Messiah's descent in the house of David, though that is true. At a deeper level, the interplay of sin and redemption which we see in this story is the reason Christ came into our world: sin and redemption.

The sin is the sin of David, who sees a pretty girl and wants her, even though he knows she's married. He gets the woman pregnant then sets up a cunning, cruel ploy to escape the consequences of what he'd done. And when Bathsheba's husband cannot be tricked into thinking that the baby is his, precisely because he is loyal, faithful, disciplined and upright, (the irony of that is brutal!) David manipulates the military and arranges to have him killed in battle.

It is a shameful tale, narrated in scripture with unflinching honesty.

(Which, incidentally, testifies to the power of scripture. David was lionized in Israel, their ideal king, and yet this story was not censored nor suppressed!)

Stories to Live By

It was not suppressed or forgotten because of its power to highlight the destructive power of sin.

This is not a topic I need to develop or discuss. We read the papers; we watch the TV news. We know sin in all its grubby, messy ugliness. The world is full of it.

But the world is also full of the love of God, our Creator and Redeemer. This story's in the Bible because as well as sin there is redemption. God did not give up on sinning David. He sent a prophet to confront David. Nathan told David a story about a rich man too mean to serve up one of his own lambs to an unexpected guest. He took the only lamb a poor neighbor possessed and served it up. David was outraged at the wrong.

And Nathan said, "You are the man;" the man who sees the injustice of a rich man taking another man's lamb and killing it, but did not see the injustice in taking another man's wife and then killing her husband.

Nathan's parable did its work. David saw the truth and repented. Seriously repented. And God forgave David his great sin. And more than that, God worked in and through the sin to advance his purpose and accomplish his plan. Bathsheba soon gave birth to Solomon who became the wisest, richest king that Israel ever had.

Notice: this is not a feel-good, 'they all lived happily ever after" kind of a story where everyone achieves the "closure" our culture always wants immediately something goes wrong. David is forgiven. Forgiveness means escape from condemnation, but not escape from the consequences.

The consequences were dire. Bathsheba joined the royal harem and the other women who bore David sons plotted and intrigued to position their sons to be the one to succeed to David's throne. Domestic turmoil led to civil war that devastated the nation. It was a terrible time in Israel.

And yet God was at work. When God's people turn to God in penitence and faith that's all God needs for God to be present and at work redemptively. It's not always immediately apparent; sometimes only hindsight makes God's actions clear, but nonetheless God is at work. Think of some of the places in scripture where God gets down and dirty in the mire of human sin to redeem and to restore, and advance his purpose.

- In Genesis, Joseph's brothers sell him into slavery and years of misery and, yet Joseph can tell them: Even though you intended to do me harm, God intended it for good …[42]
- In the Acts of the Apostles, Stephen is put to death and the church persecuted. Many Christians flee for their lives. But the scattering of the church is the scattering of the gospel and the Christian message spreads.[43]
- Supremely, of course, in Jesus. All the sin that accumulated to put him on the cross became—without in any way being diluted—became the definitive demonstration that proved God's love.

The Cambridge theologian, Harry Williams, once said

> From the point of view of the Christian faith, so completely does God make all things into the instruments of goodness that we are driven to say that had there been no Judas, no Caiaphas and no Pilate, the loss to humanity would have been irreparable.[44]

God's love works miracles like that.

We know the power of human love. You remember George Orwell's novel *1984*? In the bleak and brutal world of Big Brother, government power is absolute, and dissidents simply disappear. They don't even have to be guilty of anything, just suspected. The hero, Winston Smith, feels sure that he is next to be eliminated, and something in him dies. He becomes depressed and careless. Then

---

[42] Genesis 50:20
[43] Acts 6:1 – 8:4.
[44] H A Williams, CR, *The True Wilderness* London and New York, Continuum, 1965, 161

his friend Julia furtively slips him a note. It simply says, "I love you." Orwell writes:

> At the sight of the words 'I love you', the desire to stay alive welled up in him and the taking of minor risks suddenly seemed stupid.[45]

His situation changed. He was loved, known, cared for. Things were no longer totally hopeless. Now he had significance, he was loved.

And if that is true of our human loving, how much more is it true of the love which at Christmas brought the Christ child into a world of sin. Sin that included at Bethlehem:

- People being too busy, too self-absorbed to care—forcing the birth out into a stable;[46]
- Religious leaders too indifferent to their faith to check out the birth in Bethlehem;[47]
- A secular leader who combined an arrogant assumption of his right to rule with a cruel insecurity that sought to kill any potential threat to his power …[48]
- …forcing the holy family to flee and taste the pain and bitterness of being refugees.[49]

And Jesus enters it—the love of our redeemer God confronting our broken world. It's foreshadowed in the family tree of Jesus, and fulfilled in his life and ministry.

And so this R-rated family tree which Matthew gives of Jesus, tells stories which surprise us:

> the unexpected people who are agents for God's love, and stories of the strange and unexpected ways God works and uses them.

---

[45] George Orwell, *1984* New York: Harcourt, 1947, 105
[46] Luke 2:7
[47] Matthew 2:4-6
[48] Matthew 2:16-18
[49] Matthew 2:13, 20.

Norman M. Pritchard

There are no limits to God's love. There is room in the story of this family for all, because it's a story of sin and its redemption, of the depths of human weakness and the heights of love divine.

For God so loved the world that he gave his only Son ...

Forgiveness
Matthew 6:12, 14-15

And forgive us our debts,
as we also have forgiven our debtors.
And do not bring us to the time of trial,
but rescue us from the evil one.

For if you forgive others their trespasses, your heavenly Father will also forgive you; but if you do not forgive others, neither will your Father forgive your trespasses.

Sometimes you pick up a book and the opening sentence grabs you: you *simply must* keep reading. Like these first lines:

> I have a confession to make: I was once considered a national security threat. For months I was interrogated – not only about details of my own life but also for incriminating information about other people suspected of posing a threat to the state.[50]

This was not a Tom Clancy novel, it was theology! The author is Miroslav Volf, a great theologian who has taught at Fuller Seminary and Yale Divinity School. In 1984, Volf had been called up for military service in Yugoslavia, at that time still a communist country.

> My wife was an American citizen and therefore, in the eyes of my commanders, a potential CIA spy. I had been trained in the West in a "subversive" discipline that studies everything as it relates to God, who is above all worldly gods – including those of totalitarian regimes…

That was another black mark. Volf's Ph.D. was on Karl Marx, at that time seriously out of favor in Yugoslavia, and therefore grounds for more suspicion. Worse, his father was a pastor whom the secret police suspected of sedition and regularly harassed.

---

[50] Miroslav Volf, *The End of Memory*. Grand Rapids: Eerdmans, 2007, 3.

The soldiers in his unit spied on him. They would try to provoke him into incriminating statements. Some tried to discuss religion, a forbidden subject. He was even appointed to a normally attractive desk job, but that required him to work in a room that was bugged. He endured a year of intimidating, callous and contradictory interrogations, all accompanied by dire threats unless he confessed to what the authorities "already knew" about him.

Volf knows it could have been worse: there was on torture, no violence; but he still felt paralyzed by fear, helplessness and humiliation.

As a Christian theologian, how can Volf offer forgiveness? For over 8 years Volf has worked on a book, exploring the challenges of forgiveness: How could he remain true to what he calls, "the stance toward others that lies at the heart of the Christian faith—love of the enemy, love that does not exclude the concern for justice, but goes beyond it."?[51]

As he developed his book, three concerns were uppermost:

1. Concern for himself as the wronged person. How should he regard his suffering, and those who caused it?

2. Concern for the wider social setting: what does it mean to live in a world where such wrongs happen? And, of course, lots of people have suffered worse than he did.

3. And he was concerned about those who abused him: "what does it mean to remember rightly in regard to the wrongdoer?"

I haven't read the whole book yet, but these questions allow us to think about some of the big issues forgiveness raises.

1   Forgiveness and the wronged person.

Contrary to popular wisdom, forgiveness does not mean 'forget what's happened; it doesn't matter.' Even for casual social settings,

---

[51] Volf, 10.

that is misleading, but for serious experiences of wrongdoing, that can be disastrous.

Forgiveness is painful, because of the wrong that has been suffered, and the need to confront it. You may have been attacked, abused, unfairly treated, betrayed. The deed is done; it can't be undone. In Volf's case, that meant the loss of a whole year to paralyzing fear. It cannot be recovered, and that's a painful fact.

But how are we going to deal with that fact? We must—because the past always influences the present and the future. Are we going to leave it in the past, and rise above it; or are we going to carry it around, allowing it to continue hurting, spoiling, perhaps even distorting the life we're trying to live? That's difficult; and we don't always want to face it.

Often our first instinct is to hit back and respond either in anger or in some form of revenge. That, too, is not helpful. Volf reminds us,

> To triumph fully, evil needs two victories, not one. The first victory happens when an evil deed is perpetrated; the second victory, when evil is returned.[52]

That's why, so often, revenge and getting even end up doing more harm than good. You can make the wrongdoer feel what you have felt, but all that does is spread the pain; it will never reduce it. That is why forgiveness exists: forgiveness means giving up hope of a better past—but doing so for the sake of a better present and future.

Desmond Tutu, retired Anglican Archbishop of Cape Town, now travels the world sharing the lesson of South Africa's Truth and Liberation Commission, in which the victims of the violence apartheid spawned were allowed to tell their stories and confront their past. He tells audiences in places like Rwanda, Northern Ireland and the Middle East what they discovered in South Africa: "There is No Future Without Forgiveness," [53]

---

[52] Volf, 9.
[53] Also the title of a book. Desmond Tutu, *No Future Without Forgiveness*. New York: Doubleday An Image Book, 1999.

He cites a cartoon on the cover of the journal, *Spirituality and Health*. It shows servicemen standing at the Vietnam Memorial in Washington D.C. One asks, "Have you forgiven those who held you prisoner of war?" "I will never forgive them," replies the other. "Then it seems they still have you in prison, don't they?" [54]

It is precisely because forgiveness has let him out of the prison of his grief and loss, that the father of the prodigal runs out with joy to greet him. He's free at last! It's welcome home for *both of them*!

2. **Forgiveness and others**.

But forgiveness is never just personal, is it? Other people are always involved. For Miroslav Volf, that meant dealing with thoughts of how such things as he suffered, and worse, can go on in the world.

We all know: stuff happens, things go wrong. When we're at the giving end of wrongdoing, we're glad that there's forgiveness; but when we're on the receiving end, it isn't always easy to forgive. 94% of Americans surveyed in a Gallup poll said forgiveness was important; but only 48% said they usually tried to forgive others.[55]

We're all like the elder brother: we're so angry at what the prodigal has done wrong that we fail to see our own shortcomings. We've soiled our nest with ingratitude and soured relationships. The elder brother can't share his father's happiness—he's too busy thinking 'what about me? What do I get?' For all his goody-two-shoes demeanor, the elder brother's every bit as lost at home as his brother in the pigpen.

Even if he reverses Jesus' saying, and so can see the plank in his brother's eye, there's still a speck in his own eye, and it blinds his vision.

And the very moment of his father's joy—he's just received his lost son back again—becomes the moment of new grief—the other son's now lost! So our world is a crazy mixture of bad people doing

---

[54] Desmond Tutu, *No Future Without Forgiveness*, 272.
[55] http://www.forgiving.org/Campaign/power.asp

good things and good people doing bad things. That's why we need forgiveness!

Did you see the movie, *Crash*? *Crash* powerfully shows what can happen when different people encounter one another and clash. The movie starts off with a series of vignettes in which the characters run up against each other in everyday situations: a fender bender, language barriers in a store, an encounter on the street, a long wait at a restaurant, a traffic stop, an immigrant tradesman working on your home.... The characters say and do things better left unsaid and undone. As the movie proceeds, many of them cross paths again, and some of the characters who first appeared bad do good things, and some good characters do bad things.

Even the abusive, racist cop cares for a sick father with deep compassion, and puts his life at risk to rescue from a car wreck the very woman he had earlier assaulted! Such a mix of good and bad! As I watched it, I recalled words of Robert Louis Stevenson,

> There is so much good in the worst of us, and so much bad in the best of us, that it behooves all of us not to talk about the rest of us.

Forgiveness makes us face the truth about ourselves. We need to learn humility.

3. Forgiveness and the wrongdoer

But what about the wrongdoer? Here we see that, even though it's free, forgiveness isn't cheap.

The pain the prodigal has caused his father is eased by his return, but not erased. It's still there and in the days and weeks ahead the prodigal's going to have to live in that uneasy peace that marks attempted reconciliation, until his father's pain and his own shame subside.

He's got to deal with his brother, and who knows how that will go? But also with his father, and the servants and the neighbors, every one of whom knows what he has done; and every one of whom is watching to see how seriously he means his repentance. Did he come home because he was hungry, or because he was sorry? Do we ask for forgiveness because we repent of our actions, or regret being discovered?

I love the story George MacLeod tells at his own expense:

> I was busy. I was writing letters. I was self-important. My little daughter was going to school that morning for the first time. She came into my room, in her first school uniform. I was busy. I was writing letters. I said, "Your tie is not quite straight." Then I looked at her eyes. She wasn't crying. She was unutterably disappointed. She hadn't come for tie inspection. She had come to show me she was going to school for the first time. A terrific day. And I let her down …. I had missed the moment, missed the point. I will always see those eyes. Sometimes when I am very busy. Sometimes when I'm writing letters. I am forgiven, but I won't forget.[56]

And there's the grace. Forgiveness holds out rich possibilities:

> If I am a victim—forgiveness frees me from the past.

> If I am a broken member of a broken community—forgiveness teaches humility.

> If I am a wrongdoer—forgiveness offers new beginnings.

Show us who we are, dear Lord and who you are. Help us learn from you the art of true forgiveness and, in all our dealings, help us live in its redeeming grace; through Jesus Christ, our Lord. Amen

---

[56] Ron Ferguson, *George MacLeod*. London: Wm. Collins, 1990, 306

Take Some Humble Pie with Your Fatted Calf
Luke 15:11-32

Then Jesus said, 'There was a man who had two sons. The younger of them said to his father, "Father, give me the share of the property that will belong to me." So he divided his property between them. A few days later the younger son gathered all he had and travelled to a distant country, and there he squandered his property in dissolute living. When he had spent everything, a severe famine took place throughout that country, and he began to be in need. So he went and hired himself out to one of the citizens of that country, who sent him to his fields to feed the pigs. He would gladly have filled himself with the pods that the pigs were eating; and no one gave him anything. But when he came to himself he said, "How many of my father's hired hands have bread enough and to spare, but here I am dying of hunger! I will get up and go to my father, and I will say to him, 'Father, I have sinned against heaven and before you; I am no longer worthy to be called your son; treat me like one of your hired hands.'" So he set off and went to his father. But while he was still far off, his father saw him and was filled with compassion; he ran and put his arms around him and kissed him. Then the son said to him, "Father, I have sinned against heaven and before you; I am no longer worthy to be called your son." But the father said to his slaves, "Quickly, bring out a robe—the best one—and put it on him; put a ring on his finger and sandals on his feet. And get the fatted calf and kill it, and let us eat and celebrate; for this son of mine was dead and is alive again; he was lost and is found!" And they began to celebrate.

'Now his elder son was in the field; and when he came and approached the house, he heard music and dancing. He called one of the slaves and asked what was going on. He replied, "Your brother has come, and your father has killed the fatted calf, because he has got him back safe and sound." Then he became angry and refused to go in. His father came out and began to plead with him. But he answered his father, "Listen! For all these years I have been working like a slave for you, and I have never disobeyed your command; yet you have never given me even a young goat so that I might celebrate with my friends. But when this son of yours came back, who has devoured your property with prostitutes, you killed the fatted calf for him!" Then the father said to him, "Son, you are always with me, and all that is mine is yours. But we had to celebrate and rejoice, because this brother of yours was dead and has come to life; he was lost and has been found."'

Norman M. Pritchard

Neddy died a quiet death. Then he went not quite to heaven. He found himself in a room full of switches and dials and gadgets and screens. Then an angel appeared. His name was Fred.

"What is this place?" Neddy said to Fred.

"This is the place where you edit your life," said Fred. He reached in under his wing and pulled out a large spool of film. "This is the film of your life. Every moment, every thought, every deed good and bad."

Neddy felt cold, even though he was already dead.

"But it is too long," said Fred the Angel. "So we will let you cut it down on this machine here." Fred showed Neddy how the special editing desk worked. He taught Neddy how to add music, do lap dissolves, split screens and special effects. He then gave Neddy a big black bin in which to throw the discarded footage.

"How long can I make it?" asked Neddy, very politely.

"Normal feature-film length will do," said Fred the Angel. "And take your time. You've got plenty of it. Remember you're in eternity now. So do a good job." Then Fred the Angel left.

Neddy couldn't believe his luck. He got straight to work splicing his life and rapidly compiled what he thought was a fair picture of himself. When he finished, not too long after, he buzzed Fred the Angel.

"Here is my life," said Neddy proudly, presenting him with the final cut reel. "Tight and well-paced and all told in 98 minutes."

"You keep it," said Fred the Angel as he picked up the big black bin. "We judge by the off-cuts."[57]

Beneath the gentle whimsy of that tale, there is a powerful theological point which is, I think, profoundly Christian: we are

---

[57] "The Editing Suite" in the series "A Modern Fable" by Jim Schembri, *The Age*, Melbourne. I do not have the date.

judged by our regrets, by the quality of our repentance, by its depth, and seriousness.

Let's use that modern parable to understand the ancient one, the oh-so-familiar Parable of the Prodigal Son. It will help dispel any thought we had that that parable made forgiveness, somehow, easy, cheap, a let-off we're entitled to. Forgiveness is anything but that.

It's true: this parable might seem to teach that forgiveness is cheap and easy. Fred Craddock, preacher extraordinaire, puts it best.

> Every religion worth its salt has rites and processes for the restoration of the erring, but they are rites of sackcloth and ashes, not rings and robes, of bread and water, not fatted calf, of silence and prayer, not music and dancing.[58]

We know what Craddock means. Many times, we read the story and we think: the Prodigal got off too lightly; he ought to have been made to pay, before he was accepted back. You know, his elder brother had a point…

But if you think about the parable, you will see that this concern is unfounded. To understand forgiveness, three words are crucial; all of them begin with A: Acknowledgment—Admission—Action.

John Austin Baker once said,

> … anyone who truly wants to be forgiven must be prepared to be humiliated.[59]

He doesn't mean that the person we ask forgiveness from is going to rub our faces in our wrong and make us squirm. That sometimes happens, and it may be fair or not, depending on the situation. But there's another humiliation that is a proper, necessary humbling. It happens earlier in the process, internally, when we acknowledge to ourselves that what we've done needs to be forgiven. "When he came to himself…" the parable says.

---

[58] Fred Craddock, *The Gospels*. Interpreting Biblical Texts, series, Nashville: Abingdon, 1982, 116.
[59] John Austin Baker *The Foolishness of God*. London: Fontana 1975, 132.

Norman M. Pritchard

With no one else around, we sit in the pigsty we have gotten into and face the truth of where we are and what we've done. Gee, I've messed up. I'm in the wrong. The plans I made, the things I did—or said—they maybe weren't as smart as I had hoped. In this respect at least, I'm not the big cheese that I want to be.

And frankly, if we in any sense are serious and responsible people, that's a devastating moment: to face the truth of our mistakes. A large serve of humble pie.

I think it's because humble pie tastes so bitter that we're reluctant to face this fact: the road back—through forgiveness—starts out from this acknowledgement of what we've done.

As so often, Barbara Brown Taylor has an appropriate story.

> I recently visited an Alcoholics Anonymous group that meets in the basement of a Presbyterian church. I was there at the invitation of a young man who was celebrating his second year of sobriety. Two years earlier he almost died when he wrecked his car while he was driving under the influence of drugs and alcohol. Luckily for him, his sentence included a rehabilitation program and a long period of parole during which he became a member of A.A.
>
> The night I was there, his parents were there too … The young man spoke frankly about his self-destructiveness, his former deception of his friends and family, and the strong temptation he sometimes felt to go back to the way things were. The other people in the room nodded, knowingly. A few even reminded him of some sordid things he had done that he had left out of his narrative. More than once I wanted to jump up and clap my hands over his mother's ears—not because anyone was saying anything mean about her or her son, but simply because they were speaking the truth in her presence.
>
> She was fine with it… [Taylor was not] What am I afraid of? That someone will be revealed for who he or she is. That I

will be revealed for who I am, and that it will not be a pretty sight.[60]

A point, I think, to ponder. Our sanitized, idealized, perhaps even fantasized picture of ourselves is usually not the truth of who we are and what we're like. The first step we need to take is to acknowledge it: to face the truth of who we are. It can be deeply humiliating; however, as AA will quickly tell you, it is also deeply healing.

So acknowledge. Then admit. After you know the truth about yourself—or, at least, about your behavior—go to the person you have wronged and 'fess up. Admit, apologize, make verbal reparation. I think we often hesitate to take this step for fear of what the person we have wronged will say. We fear humiliation at her hands. But notice this: if we have done the work of acknowledgment properly, she can't humiliate us any more than we've already done ourselves!

See how this works! Without our own acknowledgment, what she might say about our bad behavior could hurt, embarrass, even anger us, and we might be goaded into hitting back: "How dare you say that about me!" or "Who do you think you are, Ms Self-Righteous?" or, "Hey, you're not so great yourself, you know. I remember once …" And suddenly attempted reconciliation becomes a battle-field and things descend from bad to worse…

But if you've done the work of self-acknowledgment, you can admit she's right. She tells it like it is and you say, "Yes, I know. Can't argue. I've faced that ugly truth about myself." The anger is defused. Its sting has gone. The healing can begin; the new relationship can start.

But only start: until now the work has been preparatory, dealing with the past. Now we face the present and the future and the third dimension of forgiveness: Action. Now we face the work of reconciliation. As John the Baptist used to tell his hearers, "Bear fruit worthy of repentance." (Mt.3:8) Action in our lives--not to earn our forgiveness, but to express it!

---

[60] Barbara Brown Taylor, *Speaking of Sin*. Cambridge, Ma.: Cowley, 2000, 80f.

When the Prodigal returned and tried to say, "Father, I have sinned … I am no longer worthy to be called your son; treat me like one of your hired hands" did he mean it? He'd better have, or his quest for forgiveness wasn't genuine. Harry Emerson Fosdick used to say that the sign of true repentance was that we didn't repeat the sin.

Let's recap: first we acknowledge the truth about our past behavior. Then we admit it and ask for forgiveness. Next, the action: we get to work to build a new relationship in which our past mistakes are warnings not to go that way again; not to say, or do, those things again. As George MacLeod once said, after his daughter had forgiven him a wretched wrong, "I am forgiven, but I won't forget."[61]

See? His serve of humble pie's still there! It's like a side-salad which he retains throughout the main course which, of course, is fatted calf, the food of celebration of forgiveness. But the humble pie's still there.

Erich Segal did my generation a huge disservice when, in his novel *Love Story*, he gave us a slogan which became proverbial: "Love means never having to say you're sorry."

That's rubbish! If that were true, it would mean that the things we do to injure love don't matter very much and the hurts we give are no big deal. And that is just not true!

If only he had said a little more:

> Love means never having to say you're sorry twice for the same mistake.

Because the pain of the wrong you've done keeps you humble and the joy of being forgiven keeps you strong—and determined not to go that way again.

---

[61] Ron Ferguson, *George MacLeod*. Glasgow: Collins, 1990, 306.

Risky Business
Matthew 25:14-30

'For it is as if a man, going on a journey, summoned his slaves and entrusted his property to them; to one he gave five talents, to another two, to another one, to each according to his ability. Then he went away. The one who had received the five talents went off at once and traded with them, and made five more talents. In the same way, the one who had the two talents made two more talents. But the one who had received the one talent went off and dug a hole in the ground and hid his master's money. After a long time, the master of those slaves came and settled accounts with them. Then the one who had received the five talents came forward, bringing five more talents, saying, "Master, you handed over to me five talents; see, I have made five more talents." His master said to him, "Well done, good and trustworthy slave; you have been trustworthy in a few things, I will put you in charge of many things; enter into the joy of your master." And the one with the two talents also came forward, saying, "Master, you handed over to me two talents; see, I have made two more talents." His master said to him, "Well done, good and trustworthy slave; you have been trustworthy in a few things, I will put you in charge of many things; enter into the joy of your master." Then the one who had received the one talent also came forward, saying, "Master, I knew that you were a harsh man, reaping where you did not sow, and gathering where you did not scatter seed; so I was afraid, and I went and hid your talent in the ground. Here you have what is yours." But his master replied, "You wicked and lazy slave! You knew, did you, that I reap where I did not sow, and gather where I did not scatter? Then you ought to have invested my money with the bankers, and on my return I would have received what was my own with interest. So take the talent from him, and give it to the one with the ten talents. For to all those who have, more will be given, and they will have an abundance; but from those who have nothing, even what they have will be taken away. As for this worthless slave, throw him into the outer darkness, where there will be weeping and gnashing of teeth."

Matthew 25:21 His master said to him, 'Well done, good and trustworthy slave; you have proved trustworthy in a few things, I will put you in charge of many things

L ife's a risky business. If we knew how risky, we'd never do a thing. We are at risk from the moment we get up in the morning, till last thing at night—and beyond. We might slip in the shower and bang our head or we might touch a live wire as we turn out the light at night or we might be sound asleep and a storm blow a tree limb through our bedroom roof.

We could be driving home at night, carefully and responsibly, and be hit broadside by someone running a red light.

I checked up risks on the internet. Wikipedia told me

> Risks can come from uncertainty in financial markets, project failures (at any phase in design, development, production, or sustainment life-cycles), legal liabilities, credit risk, accidents, natural causes and disasters as well as deliberate attack from an adversary, or events of uncertain or unpredictable root-cause.

Just as I was about to panic, the article made an important point:

> The strategies to manage risk typically include transferring the risk to another party …[62]

Like the guy whose tossing and turning in bed woke his wife up one night.

"What's wrong with you?"

"I can't sleep."

"Why not?"

"I'm worried. I owe Bob $5,000. I told him I'd repay him by tomorrow and I don't have the money."

His wife handed him the phone. "Call him. Call him right now," she said.

---

[62] Wikipedia, s.v. "Risk Management."

"But it's the middle of the night."

"Call him. Tell him you don't have the money. Let him do the worrying."

Ah yes, transfer the risk to another party!!

Today's reading is all about risk. Three slaves are given huge amounts of money while their master leaves on his travels. With all the financial meltdowns of recent years we're well aware of the risks of investing. The safer the investment, the lower return on our money.

And in those ancient days, there were no safeguards, no guarantees. The three slaves were really exposed to serious risks in investing the vast sums of money their master entrusted to them. Two turned out to be very successful: 100% return. The third feared the risks and did nothing more than preserve the capital intact.

Most of the time when we read this parable, we think it encourages us to rise to the challenge, seize the day and use the gifts that we've been given. After all the two who did that are richly praised and rewarded. There's positive encouragement to motivate us, with, for added effectiveness, the negative warning—in the dreadful displeasure of the master who throws the unprofitable servant out.

But the danger in that interpretation is that it will breed a "works righteousness," where we think we have to work and earn our way into God's favor. You know, the thinking that develops Avis Christians, Christians who adopt the car hire company's slogan: "We try harder" …

Nothing wrong with trying harder, except we know that's not the meaning of the parable. We know that from the way the parable begins. The master gives the slaves the amounts of money they are to invest. The parable starts with a detail that points us to the generosity and goodness of God and, indeed, _the risks God runs_ in entrusting anything to our care.

Norman M. Pritchard

The great German preacher and theologian, Helmut Thielicke, once called the human race "the risk of God."[63] He was thinking of the risk that lies in the freedom with which God has graced us, every step of the way. In creating us, in entrusting the world to us, and giving one another to us, in endowing us with gifts, in entrusting the great commission to the disciples, God trusts the outcome of his ventures to us, and risks his return on our effectiveness, our faithfulness.

God's risk is real, but not totally unprotected. Matthew tells us the master gave "to each according to his ability." I have two quibbles with that translation. First the word 'ability.' Matthew uses the Greek word for power, which also does mean ability. But that implies things fixed and settled, fully developed. However, the word can also mean capability, almost potential or possibility. And that opens up the thought of growth, development, enhancement. And that fits the parable's outcome. The master says to the two faithful slaves, in exactly the same words,

> Well done good and trustworthy slave. You have proved trustworthy in a few things, I will put you in charge of many things; enter into the joy of your master.

The second quibble is that there is a word untranslated in "to each according to his ability." The word is individual or personal, so that the phrase could mean "to each according to his personal capability and potential."

So back of this story are two important thoughts. First, the gifts the talents we are to use in God's service come to us from God. "What do you have that you did not receive?" Paul asked the Corinthians[64]. But secondly, these gifts are given to us, taking into account our potential, our possibilities, which we develop one step at a time, one opportunity after another.

At the men's retreat this year, we heard a story from Bill Hybels. One day he saw an elderly lady struggling to get groceries out of her car. On an impulse, he went over to help.

---

[63] Helmut Thielicke, *Man in God's World* ET: London James Clarke & Co., 1967, 147.
[64] 1 Corinthians 4:7.

It was a bigger task than he had anticipated. The grocery bags were heavy; the old lady was frail and the driveway to her apartment complex had been seal coated and was roped off and they had a long detour to reach the apartments. When he finally got the lady and her groceries home, he shook her hand to leave.

> The woman left her bony, wrinkled hand in mine long after the handshake was done. "I will believe to my dying day that God sent you to help me just now," she said.

Hybel's reaction was:

> The whole deal felt so inglorious ... the longer than expected trek, the lack of any earth-shattering results-- and yet as I walked away from the apartment complex, something in my spirit felt right. God had whispered a simple instruction my way, and this time I have actually slowed down enough to listen. There is no greater feeling in the world than to hear -- and heed -- God's voice.

Just an ordinary, everyday occurrence, the kind of thing we might not think much about after the warm glow has subsided. And yet Hybles saw a deeper meaning in it: He reflected

> I have come to believe over time that it is the little acts of obedience that invite God's power to fully flow in our lives. When you and I prove ourselves faithful with the small whispers, he entrusts us with bigger ones.[65]

Which is exactly what the parable teaches:

> Well done good and trustworthy slave. You have proved trustworthy in a few things, I will put you in charge of many things; enter into the joy of your master.

You see, we often hesitate to offer ourselves in ministry, to the church for some service that needs to be done; or to a stranger for some act of helpfulness that we could render; or to an acquaintance, for some act of witness to our faith. We're afraid of the risk of failure,

---

[65] Bill Hybels, *The Power of a Whisper*, chapter 2.

of letting God down. And we think that's being faithful and responsible.

But what if faith began elsewhere in these exchanges? What if faith began with remembering that the gifts we have are gifts from God, gifts that God wants us to use so that we grow and develop through them and realize a potential that we didn't know was there at first?

We think it all depends on us. It doesn't. It all depends on God. Jesus has done the heavy lifting and secured the salvation that gives us our faith. Then he gives us the opportunities that will grow our faith and expand our ministry and expand God's kingdom.

"In Christ," Paul tells us in 2 Corinthians, "God was reconciling the world to himself, not counting their trespasses against them, *and entrusting the message of reconciliation to us.*"[66]

Take the risk, because God already has.

---

[66] 2 Corinthians 5:19.

Whatever
Luke 10:25-37

Just then a lawyer stood up to test Jesus. 'Teacher,' he said, 'what must I do to inherit eternal life?' He said to him, 'What is written in the law? What do you read there?' He answered, 'You shall love the Lord your God with all your heart, and with all your soul, and with all your strength, and with all your mind; and your neighbor as yourself.' And he said to him, 'You have given the right answer; do this, and you will live.'

But wanting to justify himself, he asked Jesus, 'And who is my neighbor?' Jesus replied, 'A man was going down from Jerusalem to Jericho, and fell into the hands of robbers, who stripped him, beat him, and went away, leaving him half dead. Now by chance a priest was going down that road; and when he saw him, he passed by on the other side. So likewise, a Levite, when he came to the place and saw him, passed by on the other side. But a Samaritan while travelling came near him; and when he saw him, he was moved with pity. He went to him and bandaged his wounds, having poured oil and wine on them. Then he put him on his own animal, brought him to an inn, and took care of him. The next day he took out two denarii, gave them to the innkeeper, and said, "Take care of him; and when I come back, I will repay you whatever more you spend." Which of these three, do you think, was a neighbour to the man who fell into the hands of the robbers?' He said, 'The one who showed him mercy.' Jesus said to him, 'Go and do likewise.'

The lawyer's question: Luke 10:25 What must I do to inherit eternal life?

When we encounter something unfamiliar, we sometimes don't know how to react.

In Glasgow, Scotland, where I grew up, the mood in the local pub— they tell me! —can be basic and raw, mixed with a surprising friendliness. One recent lunchtime, things were very quiet. Two locals were enjoying a drink when a stranger came in, ordered, and sat in a corner by himself. One of the locals wandered over to say hello. "Where you from?" he asked. "Saskatoon, Saskatchewan," the Canadian replied.

Without another word, the Scotsman returned to his mate, who asked, "Well, where's he from?" "Dunno," his mate replied, "he doesn't speak English."

Sometimes, however, the familiar can also confound us.

What could be more familiar than Jesus' parable of the Good Samaritan? It's so familiar it's become proverbial. Hospitals, especially those that care for the poor, are named after him. Counseling centers carry his name. Everyone who makes headlines for some act of generosity or kindness gets dubbed "The Good Samaritan" in the local paper. There's nothing here we haven't heard a hundred times before: be kind ... be helpful ... be loving ... The story's so familiar we're tempted to use the teenager's blow-off phrase, "Whatever ..." and move on.

Two things, however, should give us pause, before we move on. The first thing is ourselves. Yes, the parable's familiar; it's meaning clear, perhaps even obvious. Wouldn't the world be a better place if it were filled with people who lived like that? And yet, we know, that's easier said than done.

One of the most popular preachers of today is Barbara Brown Taylor. While serving a church in rural Georgia she found the parable challenge her. It was a rainy Thursday; she was driving to church. She said, I had…

> …my seat belt on and my door locked, when I saw a car with its hood up on Howell Mill Road. As I approached, a tall black man stepped into the road, holding up a pair of jumper cables and looking me straight in the eye. Several hundred pieces of information went through my mind in about three seconds. "The man needs help—you are a single woman in a car—the man needs help—never open your door to a stranger—go to the nearest service station and send a mechanic—the man needs help—what if he cannot afford a mechanic? —the man needs help—I am sorry I

cannot help—maybe the next person will." And I drove on to work... [67]

...only to be embarrassed to remember that that week she was working on was a sermon on the Good Samaritan!!!

But another thing that should give us pause is Jesus. He doesn't usually deal in clichés or bore us with the glaringly obvious. He doesn't even nail things down for us, although we'd often wish he would.

That was what the lawyer wanted, because lawyers deal in definition, clear understanding of what's what, so that people know where they stand. The lawyer was looking for a precise, measured definition of the word, "neighbor." Definitions help us understand the boundaries, where our obligations lie—and, more importantly, where they stop.

And that's important. After all, 'love your neighbor' is complex because... well, because there are so many of them! If we're not careful, we could spend an awful lot of time loving an awful lot of neighbors and never be done. So, clarity, Jesus, please: define—who is my neighbor?

And Jesus answers, not with a definition but with a story. A man was going down from Jerusalem to Jericho ....

Stories draw us in, work on our imagination. You can read a good book, then read it again years later and find it makes a different impact on you. The story's the same; you have changed, or your circumstances, and the story yields a different meaning. Stories are lively things, living things. They invite us to identify with the situation or the characters, to empathize, to learn...

Sometimes you're the victim, beaten up by life; at other times you're busy and find it easy, necessary even, to pass by on the other side. There are even times when you stop to help and go the second mile.

---

[67] Barbara Brown Taylor, *The Preaching Life*. Cambridge, MA: Cowley Publications, 1993, 115.

It all depends. Life's full of the familiar and the unfamiliar. That's why Jesus taught in parables, not propositions. We like to think the parables are simple peasant tales from long ago, no more. No way! Have you never noticed the disconcerting way the parables have unexpected twists, surprises or leave awkward, unanswered questions?

- The shepherd did not leave his 99 sheep "safely in the fold," as the hymn piously puts it; he left them in the wilderness—at risk—while he searched for one lost sheep. Isn't that economic madness?

- Ditto the landowner who paid workers the same wage for one hour's work as he did for 12. Isn't he asking for trouble from the unions?

- And what happened at the Prodigal's welcome home party? Did his elder brother ever join the celebration? And what was the atmosphere like next day at breakfast when the neighbors had all gone and there was just the family round the table?

- In today's parable, how did the traveler on the road react when he discovered that his Good Samaritan was, well, *a Samaritan*, someone his religion taught him to despise?

See? The parables are open-ended. They leave issues hanging and invite the possibility of new responses and the exercise of unexpected gifts.

The Good Samaritan offered one response, it might not be the only one that's open to us.

Some people are managers. Perhaps we need to organize convoys so people could travel together from Jerusalem to Jericho in safety.

Others are builders. Perhaps there are dangerous spots on the road that can be made safer—smoother corners, better lighting.

Some people are politicians. Perhaps our role is to increase taxes to employ more police and keep crime down. On the other hand, reducing taxation could increase the living standards so that people did not feel the need to turn to crime ....

Whatever. Stories invite imaginative participation to see that all sorts of possibilities are open and all of them are valid ways to love our neighbor.

Jesus told stories of daily life with twists and complications to remind us: that's what God's world is like. Everything and everyone is God's. So even chance encounters can be gifts, or challenges, or opportunities from God.

The surprise in this parable is that the hero was a Samaritan, and Samaritans were despised. Today that detail rebukes us any time we marginalize people and forget their status as God's beloved children, whether we do it for racial reasons, or economic, or political ones.

This story illustrates God's preferential option for the unlikely. If a Samaritan can stand as example of eternal life behavior, then anyone can, and any loving action can.

So, we can participate in the life of God's kingdom by the way we treat the store clerk; or ignore a panhandler, the way we respond to a disaster in a country we disapprove of, or some need that was the victim's stupid fault, or whatever....

Some time ago, I saw a Good Samaritan at a filling station. He came out of a car that was throbbing to the beat of some wall bending music which almost drowned out the raucous shouts and laughter of his friends. While the driver was gassing up his car, a passenger got out and went over to help a lady struggling with the air hose to inflate her tires. He smiled, put a quarter in the slot and did her tires for her, including the spare in the trunk. She drove off without even a smile of thanks, far less a word of thanks.

Did I mention that the young men were Hispanic?

Norman M. Pritchard

The world is full of hurt and painful need, and all God needs are catalysts, to help the love of God release God's healing balm.

You see, eternal life is not waiting for us when we die; it's also here and now in every chance encounter in which we release the goodness of our God.

Lord, help me see the needs you want me to see, to react in a way that honors you, and to bless others by serving them gladly with practical expressions of your love.

It's My Party
Luke 15:1-3, 11b-32

Now all the tax-collectors and sinners were coming near to listen to him. And the Pharisees and the scribes were grumbling and saying, 'This fellow welcomes sinners and eats with them.'

So he told them this parable...

Then Jesus said, 'There was a man who had two sons. The younger of them said to his father, "Father, give me the share of the property that will belong to me." So he divided his property between them. A few days later the younger son gathered all he had and travelled to a distant country, and there he squandered his property in dissolute living. When he had spent everything, a severe famine took place throughout that country, and he began to be in need. So he went and hired himself out to one of the citizens of that country, who sent him to his fields to feed the pigs. He would gladly have filled himself with the pods that the pigs were eating; and no one gave him anything. But when he came to himself he said, "How many of my father's hired hands have bread enough and to spare, but here I am dying of hunger! I will get up and go to my father, and I will say to him, 'Father, I have sinned against heaven and before you; I am no longer worthy to be called your son; treat me like one of your hired hands.' " So he set off and went to his father. But while he was still far off, his father saw him and was filled with compassion; he ran and put his arms around him and kissed him. Then the son said to him, "Father, I have sinned against heaven and before you; I am no longer worthy to be called your son." But the father said to his slaves, "Quickly, bring out a robe—the best one—and put it on him; put a ring on his finger and sandals on his feet. And get the fatted calf and kill it, and let us eat and celebrate; for this son of mine was dead and is alive again; he was lost and is found!" And they began to celebrate.

Now his elder son was in the field; and when he came and approached the house, he heard music and dancing. He called one of the slaves and asked what was going on. He replied, "Your brother has come, and your father has killed the fatted calf, because he has got him back safe and sound." Then he became angry and refused to go in. His father came out and began to plead with him. But he answered his father, "Listen! For all these years I have been working like a slave for you, and I have never disobeyed your command; yet you have never given me even a young goat so that I might celebrate with my friends. But when this son of yours came back, who has devoured your property with prostitutes, you killed the fatted calf for him!" Then the father said to him, "Son, you are always with me, and all that is mine is yours. But we had to celebrate and rejoice, because this brother of yours was dead and has come to life; he was lost and has been found."

When my brother and I were growing up, mom would warn us when our behavior was going to get us in trouble. "You two take care. You'll go too far." We usually went too far and were punished—sent to our rooms, denied TV, or given some extra chore to burn off energy. And one of us would say, "If only we had stopped. We should have stopped."

That moment of 20/20 regret comes to people in many guises. The argument is about to be settled, one spouse is about to give in and the other says, "Well, it is just like the last time when you said …" and suddenly the argument has a whole new intensity. If only he had stopped.

Or the teenager dabbling in drugs: If only I had stopped.

Or the driver running a red light: If only I had stopped.

It's a common experience. If only I had stopped.

Ah, Jesus, Jesus. If only *you* had stopped. If only you had stopped with a simple tale of redemption—a prodigal repents and returns and is quietly forgiven, we would have accepted that. That would have been simple, safe, easy for us to accept. No matter what you've done, if you repent and come home, "We'll say no more about it." If you had only stopped at that point.

But no, you had to go on, pile on the details, stretch our understanding.

The prodigal returns, his father runs out to meet him, eagerness personified, cuts off his carefully rehearsed speech with a kiss, forgiveness personified, orders up a robe and a ring to dignify him, generosity personified, and shoes as a sign that he belongs in the family not among the slaves, acceptance personified. And then he invites the neighbors to a party with the fatted calf, hospitality personified.

Everyone must know how glad he is to have his son back. Glad? He's ecstatic, over the moon.[68] But questions arise in our minds, because we're not sure that Jesus hasn't gone too far. We find ourselves thinking that this is too easy, too glib. Come on, Jesus, forgiveness—after his behavior?

Can it really be that simple? Shouldn't the father check his son's story—probe for sincerity, lay down conditions? Ask for assurances that it won't happen again? Isn't it suspicious that the prodigal was moved to come home not by thoughts of his father but by remembering how well fed the servants were, while he starved in the pig pen …?

I think Jesus intends us to think these thoughts that reflect how we would act in similar circumstances, because he wants to provoke us, to shock us and to tell us, it doesn't matter. It's my party. This is how God is and I want you to see how desperately God loves you and how gladly he will welcome you from whatever far country you've been lost in.

Now that is challenging enough, but it gets worse. The parable is not really the Parable of the Prodigal Son. If it were, it would have begun "A certain man had a father and an elder brother…" What Jesus says is, "A certain man had two sons" and Jesus provokes us again by painting the other son as reasonably, understandably just like us.

He's the good son; responsible, conscientious. He goes to church. He stayed at home and worked the farm. Did you notice, the party was in full swing, with music and dancing full volume, by the time he came in from the fields. So he's done a full day's work before discovering the party. No wonder he's angry! I remember in Melbourne every time we read this parable, one of the men who sang in the Men's Choir would leave the service and complain that the

---

[68] Alyce McKenzie, "A Prodigal Son, An Undignified Dad: Reflections on Luke 15:11-32" Patheos, Edgy Exegesis. http://www.patheos.com/Progressive-Christian/Prodigal-Son-Alyce-McKenzie-03-04-2013?offset=1&max=1 after

elder brother got a raw deal. "I agree with him," he would say, every time. "He's right to complain."

And Jesus wants us to feel that the elder brother was right, so that he can shock us once again with his truth: it doesn't matter. "A certain man had two sons," and he loved them both and wanted them both, even though they're different. One got lost in a far country and one got lost at home.

The teaching of this parable is very close to one of the great themes of John's gospel, that the coming of Jesus to the world brought light, but also revealed the darkness. "This is the judgment that the light has come into the world and people loved darkness rather than light because their deeds were evil." (John 3:19)

Now the elder brother may look the pillar of offended respectability, but Frederick Buechner points out he is guilty of several of the seven deadly sins.

> Envy and pride and anger and covetousness, they are all there … even lust as he slavers over the harlots whom he points out the prodigal has squandered his cash on.[69]

Even so, the father wants him too, forgives him too before he asks, before he even knows there's anything to forgive, and invites him into the party.

And there's the point of the parable: "A certain man had two sons." They both got lost; one in a far country and one at home. And their father loved them both and wanted them both. The parable's about the Father, not the sons—and that's Father with a capital F.

It's all about God who rejoices and parties every time a lost child comes home, and who then agonizes every time another child resists and rejects the joy. It's the same picture of God Jesus gave in that other parable where the guests who were invited refuse to come, and

---

[69] From, Frederick Buechner, *Telling the Truth: The Gospel as Tragedy, Comedy & Fairy Tale*. Cited from Frederick Buechner Weekly Sermon Illustration, Monday March 4, 2013.

servants are told to go find anyone at all and bring them to the party. It's my party, God says and I'm going to celebrate my love.

Oh, the risk of that! The patient, persistent, relentless, untiring love of God! Can you believe it!

Can't we trust God to find ways to keep his love before the world...?

And are we any better, in our beleaguered mainline corner, trembling before the challenges we face?

I have a lovely book which tells the story of a church in London through short biographies of the pastors who had served there since 1635. A very mixed bunch, they were

> ...often worldly, often obscurantist, often baselessly authoritarian. It almost constitutes a new argument for the existence of God: if the flock could survive [pastors] like some of these, there must have been a God to guide it.[70]

And there was; and there shall be, for God is not finished with us yet. This parable speaks of the love of God which was fully revealed in the life, ministry, death and resurrection of Jesus. And if death did not stop him, we need not fear our lukewarm, inadequate faith will, either!

God's love just keeps on keeping on! And God wants us to share the joy and spread the joy!

---

[70] John Whale, *One Church, One Lord*. London: SCM Press, 1979, 163-4.

Our Undiscriminating God
Luke 16:1-13

Then Jesus said to the disciples, 'There was a rich man who had a manager, and charges were brought to him that this man was squandering his property. So he summoned him and said to him, "What is this that I hear about you? Give me an account of your management, because you cannot be my manager any longer." Then the manager said to himself, "What will I do, now that my master is taking the position away from me? I am not strong enough to dig, and I am ashamed to beg. I have decided what to do so that, when I am dismissed as manager, people may welcome me into their homes." So, summoning his master's debtors one by one, he asked the first, "How much do you owe my master?" He answered, "A hundred jugs of olive oil." He said to him, "Take your bill, sit down quickly, and make it fifty." Then he asked another, "And how much do you owe?" He replied, "A hundred containers of wheat." He said to him, "Take your bill and make it eighty." And his master commended the dishonest manager because he had acted shrewdly; for the children of this age are more shrewd in dealing with their own generation than are the children of light. And I tell you, make friends for yourselves by means of dishonest wealth so that when it is gone, they may welcome you into the eternal homes.

My wife and I went to see the movie *Sully* last weekend: you know, the movie about Captain Chesley Sullenberger's desperate but skillful and successful landing of his disabled plane in New York's Hudson River in January 2009.

We thoroughly enjoyed the movie, but left the theater feeling that the officials from the National Transportation Safety Board hadn't come across in a very good light. The movie suggested that the Safety Board's inquiry into the incident seemed determined to prove that Sully had other viable options open to him besides the river landing. They seemed eager to discount the achievement and debunk the heroics.

Inevitably, the NTSB has protested—and rightly. Their official report—on public record—praises Sully's heroic achievement that saved the lives of all 155 persons on board.

The movie's producers defend their portrayal. Director Clint Eastwood said, "The investigative board was trying to paint the picture that [the captain] had done the wrong thing." He said their presentation sought to portray the anxiety Sully and his co-pilot felt at the inquiry.[71]

Well, maybe. But I think they have joined in a pervasive cultural trend. We want our heroes big, bold, defying all odds and defeating all opposition. To build up the good guy, we need a bad guy to drag down. So hero Sully defeats the bad NTSA. It's a frequent cultural ploy.

You see it in politics. Donald Trump branded his rivals for the Republican nomination as 'losers.' Hillary Clinton consigned half of Trump supporters to a 'basket of deplorables.' The bad guy has to be terrible to make the good guy look better.

You see it on social media. The comments some people make about articles on line are frightening. Someone agrees with the article, then someone disagrees with the article, then someone disagrees with the disagreement and it gets ugly very quickly. Insults fly, disparagements multiply. It's often like that on Christian web sites, too. Lord, have mercy!

I wonder if Christians haven't fallen into this trap in the way we handle the parable we read today.

We call it 'the parable of the dishonest steward,' because, after all, the guy cheated his boss: he was dishonest. And, having labeled him dishonest, we then write the guy off—a cheat, a waster, a crook! Nothing commendable there, so let's move on.

And then it hits us: Jesus used this crook to teach us in the parable! Are we to think of Jesus praising dishonesty and, if so, what do we make of that? David Buttrick speaks for many when he writes, "The parable has embarrassed Christians for centuries."[72]

---

[71] Christine Negroni, "'Sully' Is Latest Historical Film to Prompt Off-Screen Drama" *The New York Times,* September 10, 2016, B3.
[72] David Buttrick, *Speaking Parables: A Homiletical Guide.* Louisville, Ky., Westminster John Knox Press, 2000, 210.

Norman M. Pritchard

I must admit the parable troubles me. I called this sermon God: Undiscriminating, because I thought of Jesus (and therefore the God he revealed to us) as being big enough, broad-minded enough, to use a bad guy to teach us. You know, along the lines of 'no life is entirely wasted: even the worst can serve as a dreadful warning.' After all, Jesus was not afraid to get his hands dirty, nor to rub shoulders with some unsavory types. Perhaps he modeled this story on someone he knew …?

Here's my take on the story.

The parable begins with the rich man charging his manager with squandering his money. I always assumed the manager was lining his own pocket with the boss's money; that's what crooks do. But the parable doesn't say that. After he's found out, he tampers with the accounts, reducing one customer's bill by 50%, another's by 20%. I always assumed this was the first time he'd pulled that stunt. Again, the parable doesn't say so.

What if the way he discounted the accounts after he'd been discovered was what he'd been doing all along? If, in other words, he was in the habit of giving discounts to his master's customers, and then cooking the books ….? A kind of first century Robin Hood …? Sure, it was dishonest—it amounts to theft—but it was also kind.

And that's not impossible. Today's 1% or the 0.1% of 1% are by no means modern inventions! In Jesus' day the rich could be very rich and the poor very poor, utterly dependent as tenant farmers on the rich; and highly vulnerable to exploitation and abuse. Government regulation of business practices did not exist for centuries. So, there was no protection there. And while many people today resent regulation as intrusion and interference, it's there for a reason.

So if we read the parable in that vein, the steward is on the side of the poor, seeking to relieve their poverty, perhaps even putting food on some tables, albeit at the expense of his master. Perhaps he was a first century Bernie, believing that the rich had it coming to them …?

Jesus tells us the master praised the manager because he had "acted shrewdly." I think that's an unfortunate translation. As Fred Craddock[73] notes, that's not a compliment. After all, you wouldn't like it if someone called you a 'shrewd Christian.' The word carries distasteful overtones. The Greek word's basic meaning, however, is actually sensible, thoughtful or prudent. Remember the Sermon on the Mount and 'the wise man built his house upon the rock'? Same word[74]: it conjures up thought and common sense and wisdom. Could it be that Jesus is saying that the wise use of money is not to amass wealth for oneself, but having secured your own needs, to be attentive to the needs of others? And he shocks us with that truth by making a crook our teacher.

You see, all through scripture the same warning sounds: beware of money. We need possessions, but possessions can possess us and distort us into hard, uncaring people who care only about profit. The love of money is the root of all evil, 1 Timothy 6 reminds us, and we see that truth almost daily when we open a newspaper. Think EpiPen and the size of the CEO's salary. Think Wells Fargo and the "sandbagging" (their term): more than 2 million fake accounts that got thousands of bankers fired but earned the departing manager a severance of $125 million and accolades about being one of the bank's most important leaders, "a standard-bearer of our culture" and "a champion for our customers."[75] And so on, *ad nauseam*.

Jesus knows the power of money to corrode character and disrupt community by pitting rich against poor, powerful against powerless; and he warns against it. I think that's why he says in verse 9, "And I tell you make friends for yourselves by means of dishonest wealth, so that when it is gone, they may welcome you into the eternal homes." Actually, according to the Greek, Jesus did not say 'dishonest wealth,' he said, 'unjust wealth.' There's a difference.

---

[73] Fred Cradock, *Luke Interpretation Commentary*. Louisville, Ky., Westminster John Knox Press, 1990, 191.
[74] Same word again at Luke 12:42, which the NRSV translates as 'faithful and prudent' manager.
[75] Stephen Gandel "Wells Fargo exec who headed phony accounts unit collected $125 million" Fortune *Magazine* - Monday, September 12, 2016. http://fortune.com/2016/09/12/wells-fargo-cfpb-carrie-tolstedt/?iid=sr-link1
[75] http://nassauchurch.org/nassaus-refugee-resettlement-on-npr/ gives a link to the NPR story.

Jesus means the dangers wealth brings with it—of selfishness and greed and disregard for others, especially the vulnerable.

Jesus offers an alternative: money used to make friends, only not to buy loyalty for when we'll need friends, but as generating a welcome fellowship in eternity. In other words, the best use of money, after our needs are met, is in ministry, in evangelism in healthy social justice. Jesus is suggesting that it is possible to manage possessions and money, even though money is sometimes dirty, in ways that can lead us into life with God.

There were three wonderful reports on NPR's *Morning Edition* last week. Nassau Presbyterian Church[76] in Princeton, New Jersey, has a missions group that has worked with refugees for 50 years. They offered to help resettle Syrian refugees in the U.S. and were given a special case: a family of 6 with a father badly wounded. The ministry uses congregational mission money and resources of time, talent and love.

NPR's report shared the refugees' humanity and explored their challenges: language, schools, medical care. The report throbbed with the gratitude, the joy of everyone involved.

At the end of the parable Luke adds an interesting saying of Jesus. In verse 12, Jesus speaks about our not being faithful with what belongs to another... Those words make me think that what belongs to another includes the faith heritage we have entered. It belonged to others; they passed it on to us—the freedom to worship, the privilege of prayer, scriptures in language we understand and in a variety of very convenient formats, opportunities for ministry around us every moment... the list goes on. It makes me ask myself how faithfully am I handling these gifts...?

But more specifically, we are here in Christ Church as the gift of the founding members of the congregation, many happily still active in our midst. The first ten years of Christ Church have been remarkable. It is a wonderful gift we have received. Are we being faithful in our use of it? I was thrilled when our JustImagine2

---

[76] http://nassauchurch.org/nassaus-refugee-resettlement-on-npr/

campaign included a serious commitment to missions, precisely to use our money to share the love of Jesus with others; to invest in eternal futures.

A few weeks ago, we had a group of visitors from one of our mission agencies, *Turning Points*. Sabrina, their leader told me that the heartbreaking stories that are some clients' lives are more than cancelled out by the joy of helping them find their feet, get their lives together and reach for a new and positive future.

We are to be faithful stewards. Jesus shows us a crook, not to make us look good, but to make us do good, for his sake and the sake of his hurting children

Our Discriminating God
Luke 16:19-31

'There was a rich man who was dressed in purple and fine linen and who feasted sumptuously every day. And at his gate lay a poor man named Lazarus, covered with sores, who longed to satisfy his hunger with what fell from the rich man's table; even the dogs would come and lick his sores. The poor man died and was carried away by the angels to be with Abraham. The rich man also died and was buried. In Hades, where he was being tormented, he looked up and saw Abraham far away with Lazarus by his side. He called out, "Father Abraham, have mercy on me, and send Lazarus to dip the tip of his finger in water and cool my tongue; for I am in agony in these flames." But Abraham said, "Child, remember that during your lifetime you received your good things, and Lazarus in like manner evil things; but now he is comforted here, and you are in agony. Besides all this, between you and us a great chasm has been fixed, so that those who might want to pass from here to you cannot do so, and no one can cross from there to us." He said, "Then, father, I beg you to send him to my father's house—for I have five brothers—that he may warn them, so that they will not also come into this place of torment." Abraham replied, "They have Moses and the prophets; they should listen to them." He said, "No, father Abraham; but if someone goes to them from the dead, they will repent." He said to him, "If they do not listen to Moses and the prophets, neither will they be convinced even if someone rises from the dead."'

Today we face another of the troubling parables of Jesus that Luke records: the parable of the rich man and Lazarus.

The problem with parables was best summed up by Frederick Buechner,

> With parables and jokes both, if you've got to have it explained, don't bother.[77]

This parable's pretty clear, right? A rich man does nothing to help the poor and goes to hell, the poor man goes to heaven. Pretty clearcut; if more than a little troubling for people like us. But in addition to troubling questions about wealth, this parable can serve as a test

---

[77] Frederick Buechner, *Wishful Thinking*. London: Collins, 1973

case to check whether we are willing to take the Bible seriously—and answer those critics who say we don't.

In Appendix I, you'll find the General Assembly Guidelines for how Presbyterians should read the bible. Let's apply them to this difficult text.

The scripture before nus today is a text from Jesus. Guideline #1 says,

> Recognize that Jesus Christ, the Redeemer, is the center of scripture.

The center because he's Lord; the one to whom the story of God's salvation leads and from whom it flows into the world, with its call to repentance and faith, discipleship and service. So, if Jesus is Lord, we've got to take this parable seriously. Hmm.

Guideline #2's the same: here the plain text of scripture is pretty plain; allegory or subjective fantasy won't help. The parable is what it is and it means what it says.

With guideline #3 the water gets hot.

> Depend upon the guidance of the Holy Spirit in interpreting and applying God's message.

Be careful, because the Holy Spirit is often God in dangerous mode; God messing with our hearts—the fire of Pentecost, the force that zaps Saul on the Damascus Road, the power that puts unlikely people in our way. That can be scary.

Will Willimon was once preaching at Duke Chapel and told a story of a woman in India whose child needed surgery. She couldn't afford it, but had learned that she could sell a kidney and get the money to pay for the surgery. It was a powerful illustration for Willimon's sermon.

Next morning a couple was waiting for him when he got to his study. "Oh, Oh, what did I say that ticked them off," he thought. (Pastors often do, you know!) "We were in chapel yesterday," they told him.

"Afterwards, we discussed your sermon, and last night we couldn't sleep." They handed him an envelope. "This is money we'd saved for a new car. We don't need a new car. If you can guarantee that this money will go to that woman, so that she doesn't need to sell her kidney, we want to give it to you."

Willimon was stunned. He realized that he'd gone home feeling the sermon had gone fairly well but giving it no more thought than that. But the Holy Spirit is present in worship and had stirred up this couple, and had opened their hearts to the way of Jesus in the world. The Holy Spirit does that: take care.

You see the Spirit's inspiration didn't stop when pen was put to parchment and scripture written down. The Spirit makes the living word live and that can lead to transformed lives.

Doesn't even need to be dramatic. It might even be as simple as the realization that while there's enough food to feed the world, much of it is in the trash cans of American restaurants. So perhaps from now on, when you eat out, you'll be careful about your order, perhaps selective about where you eat… The Spirit works in many different ways.

Guideline #4 says: Be guided by the doctrinal consensus of the church, which is the rule of faith. This is straightforward. From national groups like Church World Service and World Vision, through local projects like Hunger Hampers, the church has always cared about the needy in the world.

One of the fascinating things about Pope Francis, is how he has voiced Christian concern for those in need. In one of his earliest press interviews, he said,

> The culture of comfort, which makes us think only of ourselves, makes us insensitive to the cries of other people, makes us live in soap bubbles which, however lovely, are insubstantial; they offer a fleeting and empty illusion which results in indifference to others; …. We have become used

Stories to Live By

to the suffering of others: it doesn't affect me; it doesn't concern me; it's none of my business![78]

But there's more: this Pope knows about Twitter. He tweets!

- The measure of the greatness of a society is found in the way it treats those most in need, those who have nothing apart from their poverty.

The doctrinal consensus of the church is clear!

Guideline 5 reminds us to love God and to love our neighbor. Ah, but who is my neighbor, a lawyer once asked Jesus, and got the parable of the Good Samaritan as Jesus' answer. We know how that goes. Opportunities present themselves; we can make a difference any day.

There was a lovely story out of Atlanta some time ago. Shortly before her wedding, a bride-to-be cancelled, and her parents' response was to approach a hunger ministry and say, "We've got a reception for 200 going to waste. Invite your clients to the meal." 200 homeless men, women and children enjoyed their best meal for ages, and the children are important because 30% of Atlanta's homeless are children. 30%--Lord have mercy.

'It was my husband's idea,' Mrs. Fowler told the media. 'We prayed about it. And when he woke up the next morning, he said, we're going to call Hosea Feed the Hungry and ask if we can donate it to the needy … And it was such a wonderful feeling.[79]

---

[78] *God's Politics, a Blog by Jim Wallis and Friends.* "Pope Francis: We Need You in Washington, D.C." Sojourners, 09-26-2013.
http://sojo.net/blogs/2013/09/26/pope-francis-we-need-you-washington-dc
[3] http://www.dailymail.co.uk/news/article-2429617/Carol-Fowler-Family-donate-daughters-course-wedding-dinner-200-HOMELESS-people-nuptials-cancelled.html#ixzz2g7a89H6A

Norman M. Pritchard

Guideline 6 advises "earnest study… interpret the influence of the historical and cultural context in which the divine message has come."

This is good. Without this guideline we'd imagine that the parable means that the rich are going to hell and the poor to heaven, simple as that. Except it's not.

Jesus did not compose this story. You'll find a similar tale in ancient Egyptian sources. There are at least eight comparable versions among the Jewish rabbis. Christians don't have a monopoly on compassion. Jesus took a story everybody knew, to hammer home his warning about the way the love of money shrivels the soul and cuts us off from the neighbors God has given us.

Further Bible study would tell you that parables have only one point. So forget the temperature of hell and the view from heaven. Don't wonder whether a wet finger would quench a thirst in hell. This parable has one point, and it is the unforgettable conclusion:

> If they do not listen to Moses and the prophets, neither will they be convinced even if someone rises from the dead.

In other words: the teaching of scripture is clear, unambiguous, unavoidable. Even a miracle couldn't make it clearer.

Do you know there are 2,350 verses in the bible dealing with money or possessions? In the first three gospels it's 10%--1 in 10 verses and in Luke it's 1 in 7.[80]

So that takes care of guideline #7 Seek to interpret a particular passage … in light of the whole Bible. The Bible is clear: God cares for the poor; so should we.

And why? Because God wants to bless us. Wealth isolates; it generates feelings of security and superiority that cut us off from others in false self-sufficiency. Do you think it is an accident that Jesus gives the poor man's name, Lazarus, but not the rich man's? He's so wrapped up in himself, so self-contained, so isolated, that no

---

[80] Jim Wallis, *God's Politics*. San Francisco: Harper San Francisco, 2005, 212.

one knows his name. No one gets near him, and that's destructive of our humanity.

On our son Andrew's first day at elementary school, his class was having lunch in the schoolyard when one of his new class mates dropped his sandwich in the dirt. Before his friend's dismay could turn to tears (he's 5, remember) Andrew shared his sandwich with him. Thus, began a friendship that took them over half of Australia together, and survived Warwick's move to Denver, then to Auckland NZ, and now to London where he's a banker, married with two kids.

Care for others, helping people, does that. Kindness creates relationships; compassion builds community; and every caring deed rolls back the darkness and the pain. The Bible tells me so.

Save us, dear Lord, from being rich in things and poor in soul, for Jesus' sake, Amen.

They Watched Him
Mark 3:1-6

Again he entered the synagogue, and a man was there who had a withered hand. They watched him to see whether he would cure him on the sabbath, so that they might accuse him. And he said to the man who had the withered hand, 'Come forward.' Then he said to them, 'Is it lawful to do good or to do harm on the sabbath, to save life or to kill?' But they were silent. He looked around at them with anger; he was grieved at their hardness of heart and said to the man, 'Stretch out your hand.' He stretched it out, and his hand was restored. The Pharisees went out and immediately conspired with the Herodians against him, how to destroy him.

Mark 3:2 They watched him to see whether he would heal him on the sabbath ...

Picture an ordinary Sunday morning. People are walking from their cars to church and they're mingling in the Narthex. Some go straight into the sanctuary without a word; others stop for a chat with a friend. Judy's mother has been ill and Elizabeth stops her to ask how she's doing. John reminds the Chair of the Property Committee that they have still not replaced the broken sign in the parking lot, the Conners carry in the cookies they have brought for coffee hour and the Klemper family come running in because they're always late. A typical Sunday morning; service will soon begin.

Now, allow for differences in day and culture and that's the kind of day it was in the story we read this morning. People have come to synagogue the way we come to church. For an ordinary act of worship.

And suddenly, it's not ordinary anymore. Jesus is brought face to face with a man who has a withered hand, and there's a sharp, collective intake of breath--people notice and stop what they're doing to watch. Very quickly, Jesus and the man are standing in the middle of a circle. And Mark says, they watched him to see whether he would heal him on the sabbath day.

Now, freeze that picture and look at their faces. Try to read in their expressions what they're thinking as they watch to see what's going to happen. Those people in the crowd—how are they watching him?

There's a group who watch with hostility and criticism. Mark specifically names the Pharisees and Herodians, but no doubt there are others too. People who know the law and who know that the sabbath can't be broken. Surely Jesus won't do a healing on the sabbath day…? But he's standing there with the man before him, as though he's about to do something. So their eyes narrow and their brows furrow, and they watch Jesus from an attitude of hostility and suspicion.

Others are curious, perhaps even excited. These are ordinary members of the congregation. Some have heard that Jesus is gaining a reputation as a healer, and they're excited that they might get the chance to see him in action for themselves. Wouldn't that be something to talk about over brunch? So they watch with curiosity.

Then there's a group of one: the man in need and this is a big moment in his life. He knows things could be utterly different with Jesus' help, so he just stands there, his heart pounding, his eyes all pleading, watching Jesus and hoping that he is going to help.

There's also a group of people seeking leadership. The disciples have been with Jesus long enough by now to know that they never know what he's going to do next. They wake up each day and say, I wonder what we'll see today? So here, they watch their master, wondering what he'll do, and how they will fit it into their understanding of God and God's way that he is radically rearranging.

Four attitudes: hostility, curiosity, need and seeking. All very different and all very real. Then and now. Some things never change! The interesting thing is that today Jesus provokes exactly the same range of attitudes in people.

There are plenty of critics around these days, from aggressive atheists to departing disciples. One of the worrying things is that while Jesus was criticized for doing more than people expected, stretching their concept of God and God's purposes to higher levels, today the followers of Jesus attract criticism for the opposite: we fail to live up to the way of Jesus.

Did you see the recent news item that according to the latest Gallup poll, the number of Americans who have faith in organized religion is at an all-time low? The report says,

> Only 44 percent of Americans today have a lot of confidence in organized religion, compared to 66 percent in 1973 when organized religion or church was the highest rated institution in Gallup's "confidence in institutions measure."[81]

Remember the criticisms the novelist Anne Rice leveled at us, when she renounced the name 'Christian'? Anne Rice called Christians:[82] "anti-gay…anti-feminist…anti-artificial birth control …anti-science…anti-life." And the truth is, that is an adequate description of what Christians are a lot of the time.

So we have to live our faith in the face of such hostility.

Other people show curiosity. As Hans Kung says, Jesus "is obviously still for innumerable people the most moving figure in the long history of [hu]mankind."[83]

You encounter it when a colleague at work asks a question with religious overtones; or when someone asks you which church you go to, and why. And an opportunity beckons to put in a good word for Jesus. People are curious.

I met Charles Colson, of Watergate fame, once. It was just a few years after Watergate and his account of how Jesus had changed his life, *Born Again*, was being widely read. He came to Melbourne for a public rally that was held in Scots Church. Now you need to

---

[81] "http://www.gallup.com/poll/155690/Confidence-Organized-Religion-Low-Point.aspx?utm_source=tagrss&utm_medium=rss&utm_campaign=syndication"
[82] Tim Rutten, "Walking Away from Christianity." Los Angeles Times, August 4, 2010. http://articles.latimes.com/2010/aug/04/opinion/la-oe-0804-rutten-20100804
[83] Hans Kung, *On Being a Christian*. ET New York, Doubleday 1976, 145.

understand that while Melbourne is one of the world's most wonderful cities, it is not wonderfully religious! It is in many ways quite a secular place.

And yet, on a Saturday night, over 1000 people crowded into church to hear him. Most of them were young and anything but a church crowd. No doubt his notoriety helped, but what struck me was the proof that the world is still curious to see in a changed life, the evidence for Christ at work, the signs that faith is real.

And people are often curious because they feel a sense of need within them. Life is empty, somehow, unsatisfying. There must be more ... They need more.

Sometimes this need shows up when success turns sour or when things go wrong. The spate of recent shooting atrocities--at the Sikh temple In Wisconsin, the theater in Colorado, the shopping mall in Arizona and all the others since then--is a matter of growing concern, not restricted to this country.

Alan Roxburgh, a professor at Fuller Seminary, Ca., was in England a few years ago when there was a horrible series of senseless murders over the space of a few weeks. The media was full of experts offering analysis and proposing solutions. He recalls watching a morning talk show on television where a member of the panel, a man in his early 50s, interrupted the experts to ask:

> What has happened to us? How did we get here? When I was growing up as a young boy, we did lots of things that were wrong, but nothing like this. Back then [he's talking about the late 50s and early 60s], we all lived inside a way of knowing what was right and wrong. We all knew the story of Jesus, and there was a Christian background. It didn't mean we went to church, but we all knew the same story. These kids today have nothing like that anymore! There's no common story shaping us. How did that happen?[84]

---

[84] Alan J Roxburgh *Missional Map-Making – Skills for Leading in times of Transition*. San Francisco: Jossey Bass, 2010, ix-x.

You see what he means when you observe:

- the partisan intransigence of our politics
- the anger of our public debates;
- the corruptions in our institutions;
- the fragility of our relationships
- the trash that is entertainment and the deep alienation pulsing in much popular music.

Our culture, our society, shows signs of desperate need.

And there's the challenge for contemporary disciples of Jesus.

Like many 30-somethings these days, the Christian blogger Micha Boyett knows all about how unattractive the church appears to her peers. She writes,

> How many times have I cringed inside when conversations with new people in my life turn spiritual and I have to define myself through my beliefs? I'm not ashamed to confess my belief in Jesus Christ. But I am often ashamed to use the word: "Christian." What baggage does it carry in the minds of my nonbelieving friends?

Boyett understands people who want to jettison the term 'Christian' and call themselves 'Christ-follower.' But she won't go there. Because while the Christian church has done a lot of bad things, there is another side that she can't forget and won't give up. She knows Christians who live their faith, who serve others in Jesus' name.

She has friends who minister to some of the most broken of the poor in San Francisco, and some of the life changes they see are breathtaking.

But there are less spectacular stories, too. Boyett says there's something of the "Every-girl" in the …

> … suburban high school girl who believes her only value is in her own success (whether it's in the classroom, in

athletics, in the eyes of her demanding parents, or in the label she's given by the boys she longs to impress). I also know the beauty of the moment when that girl recognizes that she is loved unconditionally by a God who knows her deepest longings. The achingly heavy weight on her back falls to the ground and she actually believes she is valuable simply because her Creator knows her and chooses her.

Who told her that such a love exists? Christians did.[85]

That's what the world needs: the healing, transforming love of God, generously spread by the followers of Jesus. And the more closely we watch Jesus and learn from him, the more we can be such followers and show that our faith can make a difference in the world.

---

[85] Micha Boyette, "Why I call myself a Christian" Patheos. Accessed at www.patheos.com/blogs/michaboyette/2010/08/why-I-call-myself-a-Christian/

Unreasonable Faith
Mark 2:1-12

"When he returned to Capernaum after some days, it was reported that he was at home. So many gathered around that there was no longer room for them, not even in front of the door; and he was speaking the word to them. Then some people came, bringing to him a paralyzed man, carried by four of them. And when they could not bring him to Jesus because of the crowd, they removed the roof above him; and after having dug through it, they let down the mat on which the paralytic lay. When Jesus saw their faith, he said to the paralytic, "Son, your sins are forgiven." Now some of the scribes were sitting there, questioning in their hearts, "Why does this fellow speak in this way? It is blasphemy! Who can forgive sins but God alone?" At once Jesus perceived in his spirit that they were discussing these questions among themselves; and he said to them, "Why do you raise such questions in your hearts? Which is easier, to say to the paralytic, 'Your sins are forgiven,' or to say, 'Stand up and take your mat and walk'? But so that you may know that the Son of Man has authority on earth to forgive sins" —he said to the paralytic— "I say to you, stand up, take your mat and go to your home." And he stood up, and immediately took the mat and went out before all of them; so that they were all amazed and glorified God, saying, "We have never seen anything like this!"

Most children in Scotland grow up knowing the story of King Robert the Bruce and the spider. Early in the 14th century, after six defeats at the hands of his English enemy, the king sat despairing in a cave (or maybe a hut?) and watched a spider attempt to attach its web to a wall (or a beam) across a gap. Six times the spider tried and failed before succeeding on the seventh attempt. This inspired Bruce to make his seventh attempt. He took to the field again, and was victorious! Perseverance rewarded against all reasonable expectation.

Our gospel reading today, of the paralyzed man dropped through the roof for healing, brings that story to mind. Surely, for the four men carrying their friend to go to such extremes, it had to be a case of one final attempt.

- Perhaps they'd missed the opportunity, last time Jesus was in town?

- Perhaps they were so tired of seeing their friend denied, and devalued that they resolved to do something about it.

So they brought their friend to Jesus. And then, when the crowds were too dense for them to reach Jesus, that was one final straw that they would not allow to break the camel's back. So, like the spider, they made one more attempt. They dug through the mud and branches which sat on the roof beams of the house where Jesus was[86] and allowed their friend to drop in on Jesus and receive his healing.

Don't you think that was rather unreasonable—interrupting Jesus, damaging someone's property? They surely didn't need to do that! If they'd only waited for Jesus to finish teaching, their friend would probably have got the attention he required. That would be the normal, conventional way to deal with that situation, don't you think?

I rather think that that's how I'd have been: safe, conventional, reasonable ... and it may be for me and people like me that Mark has included this story in his gospel. Because we need to be reminded that there's something about the Christian faith that is unsafe, risk-taking, even unreasonable. Don't you think?

Remember what George Bernard Shaw called his "Maxims for Revolutionists," which he included in his book, *Man and Superman*. One of them states,

> Reasonable people adapt themselves to the world. Unreasonable people attempt to adapt the world to themselves. All progress, therefore, depends on unreasonable people.

---

[86] Archaeologists have actually uncovered a house in Capernaum which bears signs of 1st century Christian worship. It may have been Simon Peter's house. It's roof beams were spaced in such a way as to require branches and mud to provide complete covering, exactly as Mark's account requires. See John J Rousseau and Rami Arav, *Jesus and his World*. Minneapolis: Fortress Press, 1995, 45.

Actually, that's the meaning of the story of the Christian faith: progress depends on the unreasonable.

- It was surely unreasonable to expect much of the followers Jesus left behind after Easter. Remember, they were the nobodies who'd failed almost every test they'd faced when Jesus was with them. What chance with him gone? And yet the unreasonable outcome won.

- It was surely unreasonable to expect the little church to survive after the Roman Empire turned its formidable might against it, in persecution after persecution? Again, the unreasonable outcome won.

- Martin Luther: one man's opinion against the total wisdom of Christendom. Who won? The unreasonable one won.

On and on it goes.

- It was unreasonable to expect that the faith could survive the 20th century persecution behind the Iron Curtain, "perhaps the worst in numbers of Christians the world has ever known."[87] And yet, again, the unreasonable outcome won.

- Albert Schweitzer was unreasonable, sacrificing career for mission work.

- Dietrich Bonhoeffer was unreasonable.

- Martin Luther King was unreasonable.

- Rosa Parks was unreasonable.

- Nelson Mandela was unreasonable.

---

[87] Michael Bourdeaux, *Risen Indeed—Lessons in Faith from the USSR*. London: Darton Longman and Todd, 1983,14.

- Rick Warren was unreasonable—I mean, a bible study of 7 people meeting in his condo: how could that grow into a church with 20,000 in attendance each weekend, and training over 350,000 pastors and church leaders in 120 countries… and those numbers still growing? Talk about an unexpected and unreasonable outcome!

The more you trace the unexpected progress of the Christian faith—the unreasonable progress against all reasonable expectation, you more you come to realize, it all begins with Jesus. These four men in the gospel story were unreasonable because Jesus is unreasonable. He refuses to be held back or constrained by what is reasonable.

The only way those four people could have dared attempt the risk of going in through the roof was if they knew the sort of person they were dealing with in Jesus. From listening to him, perhaps, or from listening to other people tell about him, they must have known that he would not reject them and leave their friend unhelped. Jesus is like that!

But I rather think that even they had little notion just how unreasonable Jesus could be.

The simple thing, the reasonable thing, would be to do whatever minimum was required to get the job done. Heal the man and let them all get on their way. But Jesus acknowledges, the easy way is not the way for him. "Which is easier," he asks, "to say to the paralytic, 'Your sins are forgiven,' or to say to him, 'Stand up and take your mat and walk'?

He deliberately provokes a controversy to show that the loving way, the God-like way is not the easy way, but the way that deals with the problem and brings the love of God to bear.

It seems the man's paralysis was not the problem, but the symptom of the problem. The problem was some unresolved issue in his life that had become an unbearable burden: perhaps a wrong he had committed, a relationship gone sour, some dishonesty, an injustice, a betrayal. Who knows what it was. But, whatever it was, there was some deep and heavy burden on his heart.

And at a time when people simplistically drew a straight line between sin and punishment, and believed that God punished you every time you did something wrong, it isn't hard to see how the burden of his guilt, whatever he had done, had, first metaphorically then literally, crippled him and added helplessness to the pain he suffered from.

All of which, Jesus saw. And while it would be a reasonable approach to take the line of least resistance, that is never Jesus' way. He wants to offer, not what we want, but what we need.

And perhaps, like the man in the story, there is some need over which we've given up trying.

How many times in our lives does it happen that we give up because we think it's the only reasonable thing to do?

- 'You can't change human nature' we reason, and so we give up hoping for reconciliation, or trying to be better Christians.

- 'You can't undo the mistakes of the past,' we reason, and then conclude we're going to have to live with failure.

Could it be that you've come to church today so that Jesus can be the spider in your cave: inspiring one more attempt, this time with Jesus' help, to put things right; or to make amends, or to seize the promise of forgiveness and a new beginning? You know that's what he wants.

Or perhaps you've come because you want to make a difference in the world; but the problems are too great, and you don't think there is anything you could do. Think again.

Gene Cotton is a Christian singer-songwriter in Tennessee. His wife brought home a story she'd heard in her school cafeteria about an 83-year-old woman who had just buried the grandson she had brought up since infancy. Her grief was compounded by worry that she could not pay the funeral expenses. Cotton called the funeral home. They were sympathetic and would reduce the bill by 25% if he could come up with the balance in 2 weeks. He called some churches. He called some friends. Donations came in and before the two weeks were out, the bill was paid, and Christian caring brought Christian love and joy that many people shared.[88]

Read your bulletin today: there are several places where a gift like that's on offer.

Or perhaps your Christian life is in a rut: it seems you're going nowhere; you're not sure how your faith can make a difference in your life. It's simple. Follow Jesus. Do what he requires, even if it seems unfair, unreasonable, and inconvenient.

While she was still single, Lauren Winner said that, as a new Christian, she found the issue of discipleship

> ... comes up in my life surprisingly often. Here's a recent instance:
>
> It's late, I've had a few glasses of wine, and my (male) friend and I have just finished watching an old Cary Grant film. Can't I spend the night in his apartment, so long as "nothing happens?" If I stop to think about the 13-year-old I'm mentoring at church, if I stop to think about setting an example...—the answer might, maybe, be no. Which is an annoying answer.[89]

Just as Jesus resisted the easy way, there are times when his followers do too, for his sake:

> the faithful way, not the convenient way. It may be unreasonable, but it is effective.

Checking on the details of the Rick Warren story, I came across this comment Warren once made:

---

[88] Gene Cotton, "God's Yes!" *The Upper Room Disciplines 2006*. Nashville. The Upper Room, 2005, 57.
[89] Lauren B Winner, "Diving Manifestations. Living by the Word. Sojourners, Jan-Feb 2003. Accessed at
http://www.sojo.net/index.cfm?action=magazine.article&issue=soj0301&article=030149

Christ doesn't expect us to produce *more* than we can, but he does expect us to produce *all* that we can by his power within us.[90]

His power within us. Isn't that what Mark wants us to see in the story before us?

---

[90] Rick Warren, *The Purpose Driven Church*. Grand Rapids: Zondervan, 1995, 65.

Risen Indeed
Acts 9:1-20

Meanwhile Saul, still breathing threats and murder against the disciples of the Lord, went to the high priest and asked him for letters to the synagogues at Damascus, so that if he found any who belonged to the Way, men or women, he might bring them bound to Jerusalem. Now as he was going along and approaching Damascus, suddenly a light from heaven flashed around him. He fell to the ground and heard a voice saying to him, 'Saul, Saul, why do you persecute me?' He asked, 'Who are you, Lord?' The reply came, 'I am Jesus, whom you are persecuting. But get up and enter the city, and you will be told what you are to do.' The men who were travelling with him stood speechless because they heard the voice but saw no one. Saul got up from the ground, and though his eyes were open, he could see nothing; so they led him by the hand and brought him into Damascus. For three days he was without sight, and neither ate nor drank.

Now there was a disciple in Damascus named Ananias. The Lord said to him in a vision, 'Ananias.' He answered, 'Here I am, Lord.' The Lord said to him, 'Get up and go to the street called Straight, and at the house of Judas look for a man of Tarsus named Saul. At this moment he is praying, and he has seen in a vision a man named Ananias come in and lay his hands on him so that he might regain his sight.' But Ananias answered, 'Lord, I have heard from many about this man, how much evil he has done to your saints in Jerusalem; and here he has authority from the chief priests to bind all who invoke your name.' But the Lord said to him, 'Go, for he is an instrument whom I have chosen to bring my name before Gentiles and kings and before the people of Israel; I myself will show him how much he must suffer for the sake of my name.' So Ananias went and entered the house. He laid his hands on Saul and said, 'Brother Saul, the Lord Jesus, who appeared to you on your way here, has sent me so that you may regain your sight and be filled with the Holy Spirit.' And immediately something like scales fell from his eyes, and his sight was restored. Then he got up and was baptized, and after taking some food, he regained his strength.

There's a little guy in elementary school and his teacher says to him, "How do you spell receive?" "R-E-C-I-E-V-E." "No, that's wrong," she corrects. "It's R-E-C-E-I-V-E.' "Maybe so," the lad replied, "but you asked me how I spell it."!!

Sociologists call that 'solipsism,' the self-contained mindset that sees yourself as the center of all things. Aleksandr Solzhenitsyn, the great Russian dissident and author, said our "characteristic weakness" was "learning only from [our] own experience, so that the experience of others passes us by."[91]

That comment came into my mind when I read the topic for our Daily News study and discussion session today. It concerns religious liberty in the United States, and the feeling many people have that Christians have it tough today. The article cited research findings[92] released last month:

> A growing number of Americans believe religious liberty is on the decline and that the nation's Christians face growing intolerance.
>
> - 63 percent say Christians face increasing intolerance, an increase from 50 percent in 2013.
> - Equally, 60 percent say religious liberty is on the decline, up from 54 percent in 2013.

What lies behind those statistics is the fact that our culture is becoming more diverse, more secular, and society in general is becoming less accommodating of the Christian standards that used to be at least implicit in national life.

I understand the disappointment those statistics illustrate, but I'm not discouraged because, legally, nothing has changed; none of our rights have been removed, and prickly defensiveness and whining does nothing to commend the faith to the people around us.

We need to remember the experience of others, as Solzhenitsyn said, and learn from that.

For example, while we were enjoying the celebration of Easter two weeks ago, a bomb killed 69 people in Lahore, Pakistan, injured

---

[91] Aleksandr Solzhenitsyn, One Word of Truth The Nobel Prize Speech. London: The Bodley Head, 1972, 14
[92] Bob Smietana: "Survey: Americans Say Christians Face Intolerance, but Complain Too Much: Lifeway Research, March 30, 2016.
http://lifewayresearch.com/2016/03/30/religious-liberty-on-decline/

hundreds more and was specifically targeted against Christians. And it was one of a number of recent such attacks that have killed more than 100 Christians. Attacks like that are spreading in many places in the strife-torn Middle East and the increasingly precarious Africa.

But that pattern has appeared again and again in history. At the center of our faith, of course, is the suffering and then vindication of Jesus, God's Son. The hymn we have just sung dates from the 7th century and in it John of Damascus, the great philosopher and hymn writer of the Greek Church, ties both testaments together by making connection between God's delivering of Jesus from the grip of death and God's liberation of Israel from oppression in Egypt.

> *Come ye faithful raise the strain of triumphant gladness*
> *God has brought forth Israel into joy from sadness.*
> *Loosed from Pharaoh's bitter yoke Jacob's sons and daughters,*
> *Led them with unmoistened foot, through the Red Sea waters.*
> *'Tis the spring of souls today, Christ hath burst his prison,*
> *And from three days sleep in death as a sun hath risen.*
> *Now rejoice, Jerusalem, and with true affection*
> *Welcome in unwearied strains Jesus'* resurrection. [93]

The things of God are always facing opposition in the world. Our challenge is to remain faithful, to sustain our witness and to keep the faith that God has not abandoned and will not abandon his people or his realm.

One of the privileges of my ministry arose when my last congregation established a twinning relationship with the Central Baptist Church in Moscow. Founded in 1882, the fact that it still flourishes—that it survived the 20th century—is, like the survival of Christianity in Russia after the 20th century, nothing short of a miracle of God's grace.

In the 20th century the Russian Christians suffered state harassment and persecution which brought death to many thousands of Christians and caused the wholesale closure of churches. Most were destroyed or converted to other uses.

---

[93] "Come Ye Faithful Raise the Strain" Hymn 115 in *the Presbyterian Hymnal 1990*.

Norman M. Pritchard

Under Stalin, 130,000 Orthodox priests were arrested and sent to prison camps, where 95,000 died or were executed. The number of Orthodox Churches in the Russian Republic fell from over 29,500 to less than 500.

Individual Christians suffered: their children could be taken away from them if the practiced Christianity at home or they might forfeit their jobs. Would you be a member of the church, if membership carried risks like that…?

Despite that, the church has survived and emerged with new strength and vitality today, even amid the uncertainties caused by Vladimir Putin's inscrutable policies. Central Baptist doesn't maintain a membership roll—they can't be confident the state won't turn against them again, and harass or imprison Christians.

The survival of the church under these conditions, leading to its revival after the second world war and its growth especially among intellectuals and young people today, is a miracle.

The strength of the church lies quite simply in this: that Russian Christians have been faithful to what they believe, have been willing, if necessary, to suffer for it and God has faithfully sustained them.

As part of my orientation for involvement with the Russian Church, I turned to a book I had read some years earlier, called *Risen Indeed* by Michael Bourdeaux of Keston College, an organization set up in the west to monitor the fate of Christians behind the Iron Curtain. Bourdeaux wrote,

> One day a book will be written on religion in the Soviet prison camps. It will show that when a human being is systematically deprived of everything which is normally considered his by right—family, home, work, a basic diet—at that time the influence of the Christian faith is at its most powerful.[94]

---

[94] Michael Bourdeaux, *Risen Indeed, Lessons in Faith from the USSR*. London: Darton Longman and Todd, 1983, 87.

Bourdeaux provides many examples of the impact faithful Christians had in prison camp, one of the most powerful comes from a man by the name of Vasili Koslov. He had been imprisoned for some criminal behavior and encountered Christians in prison.

> Among the general despair, while prisoners like myself were cursing ourselves, cursing the camp, the authorities and everything in the world, while we were slitting open our veins and stomachs or hanging ourselves, the Christians did not despair. They were shining with a spiritual beauty. Their pure, upright life, their deep faith and devotion to God, their gentleness and their wonderful manliness became a shining example of real life for many thousands of prisoners. One could see Christ reflected in their faces. I too wanted to live just such a pure life with high ideals… Their bonds and sufferings have turned the attention of many to Christ ….[95]

There was a similar example in our New Testament reading today. Notice again, God's faithful people under persecution. Saul of Tarsus is determined to stamp Christianity out and is prepared to travel over a hundred miles to do so. On the road he encounters the Risen Christ and just before we can say 'And the rest is history,' notice the practical detail: Saul needs to be introduced to the Christian community. Someone has to vouch for him.

God has a faithful Christian in Damascus called Ananias, and he's been awaiting Saul's arrival with some trepidation; he knows Saul's persecuting intent. But God tells Ananias to go to Saul and minister to him. Ananias protests … but Ananias is faithful.

And Luke beautifully describes what follows. In verse 17: "So Ananias went…"

He faithfully did what he believed to be God's bidding and his Christian duty. He could never have imagined the outcome, or the incredible, irreplaceable role Saul would play when he became Paul, the Christian missionary and theologian par excellence. Ananias

---

[95] Bourdeaux, 91-92.

went. He fulfilled his Christian duty. He did what was required of him and believed that he could trust God to be at work.

I am profoundly challenged by a comment Michael Bordeaux made about Soviet Christianity,

> Usually Christianity does not need to evangelize: it just needs to be itself.[96]

That is not a recipe for lazy Christianity; it is a blueprint for confident Christianity. It is the calling of Christians who are alive to the meaning of our Easter faith that the God who raised Jesus from the dead is our God, the God who brings life out of death, light out of darkness, victory out of defeat. He is the God whose faithfulness never fails.

So, in the face of discouragement, don't lose hope; in response to difficulty, don't lose heart. Keep the faith and rejoice: The Lord is risen; he is risen indeed!

Lord Jesus, whom the cross could not deter nor the grave defeat, give faith and faithfulness to your people living in difficult times and in dangerous situations, and keep us alert to our calling in the world and Christ's promise to be with us to the end. For your love's sake, Amen.

---

[96] Bourdeaux, 98.

This Life and the Next
Luke 20:27-38

Some Sadducees, those who say there is no resurrection, came to him and asked him a question, 'Teacher, Moses wrote for us that if a man's brother dies, leaving a wife but no children, the man shall marry the widow and raise up children for his brother. Now there were seven brothers; the first married, and died childless; then the second and the third married her, and so in the same way all seven died childless. Finally, the woman also died. In the resurrection, therefore, whose wife will the woman be? For the seven had married her.'

Jesus said to them, 'Those who belong to this age marry and are given in marriage; but those who are considered worthy of a place in that age and in the resurrection from the dead neither marry nor are given in marriage. Indeed, they cannot die anymore, because they are like angels and are children of God, being children of the resurrection. And the fact that the dead are raised Moses himself showed, in the story about the bush, where he speaks of the Lord as the God of Abraham, the God of Isaac, and the God of Jacob. Now he is God not of the dead, but of the living; for to him all of them are alive.'

"Some Sadducees," Luke tells us— "those who say there is no resurrection"—ask Jesus about the life to come.

Seems illogical doesn't it. It would be like President Obama asking a question about small government, or Ted Cruz asking about climate change. The objection is obvious: "If you don't believe, why do you want to know?"

Luke tells us why the Sadducees wanted to know. Their question is one of a series of questions asked by people Luke calls "spies who pretended to be honest in order to trap [Jesus] in what he said…" (verse 20.) So our reading today is like a modern political debate when one politician tries to goad an opponent into saying something that he can later use in an attack ad.

It is important to interpret this passage in the light of that context. Jesus is not giving the definitive interpretation of the afterlife; he is fending off an attack. We will only understand this passage properly if we remember two things: first the immediate context of this passage and then, secondly, the wider context of Jesus' message, and, indeed, his life.

The system the Sadducees refer to, levirate marriage, operated as the example given illustrates although, obviously, the example was ridiculous and was intended to be ridiculous. The idea was to keep a person's family name alive by having a dead man's brother produce children who would bear the dead man's name. Incidentally it also protected widows by offering security of a new husband, although the example cited reduced the woman to a possession, passed from one brother to another with the sole objective of procreation.

This scenario, and only this scenario, is in view when Jesus answers. Jesus tells the Sadducees that life in the hereafter is of a different order. People live eternally; therefore, the need to have a name perpetuated through children has gone. You won't need to make babies in heaven, to preserve your name. God makes you children of God, children of the resurrection. A new way of being! Resurrection life.

Jesus is not saying that precious relationships that have enriched our life on earth don't matter and won't matter in eternity. Actually, his reference to God as the family God—the God of Abraham, Isaac and Jacob implies the importance of family relationships in the new dimension which is God's gift to those who are blessed to receive it.

The Sadducees didn't see that, because they didn't want to see it. They wouldn't see beyond the realities of this world. They are not alone. When I was in Melbourne, a family posted a death notice in the newspaper when their father died, expressing this sad hope: May you find in heaven the things you loved on earth—a betting shop, football replays and a glass of cold beer.

There's a warning there for all of us: If you're going to ask someone to speak about you at your funeral, chose someone who is not theologically illiterate. That way you'll spare your family embarrassing, fatuous nonsense about dad playing golf on the heavenly fairways, or enjoying a martini at the divine 19th hole, or grandma greeting mother at the pearly gates with her renowned chocolate decadence dessert!

These things don't belong in the next life; they belong in this life—enjoy them here and now. Indeed, I think we ought always to be more intentional about both enjoying and appreciating the good gifts God gives us here on earth, including the family and loved ones who share our days.

There can't be many situations of bereavement where the pain of loss is not complicated by some stab of regret that we were not more attentive, more caring, more present to the one we've lost. The way to handle that regret is to deal with it here and now while there's time. I'm coming to see that the cultivation of a spirit of awareness and gratitude may be an important piece of preparation for the life to come.

The life to come will be different—that is the important, permanent point that Jesus clearly teaches here, and it fits in exactly to the second tool we use to interpret this story: the wider context of our Savior's life and teaching.

Think of the resurrection stories in the gospels. Every one of them include a note that, at first, the disciples didn't recognize Jesus—he was different, although then they came to see he was also the same. One moment he tells Mary in the garden, don't cling to me; later he invites Thomas to touch his wounds. In one story he eats a breakfast of broiled fish, in another he appears in a house even though the doors were locked. That defies analysis.

"I am the resurrection and the life," he said in John 11. "Those who believe in me, even though they die, will live, and everyone who lives and believes in me will never die," stretching the capabilities of our minds to analyze and define. Paul tried in 1 Corinthians 15, with the analogy of the plant that grows from the seed–utterly different, even though there is continuity. Perhaps Paul's best word on the subject comes in 1 Corinthians 2:

Scripture speaks of 'Things beyond our seeing, things beyond our hearing, things beyond our imagining, all prepared by God for those who love him.'[97]

---

[97] 1 Cor.2:9, REB. Perhaps citing Isaiah 64:4 (REB footnote ad. loc.)

Beyond our seeing, but not beyond our attaining. I don't mean that we are to work our way to heaven and earn our place there. When Jesus says in verse 35 "those who are considered worthy of a place in that age ..." he means 'those whom God considers worthy' and that means those in whom God sees faith in Jesus Christ and faithful living in the way he taught: loving God heart, soul, mind and strength and loving neighbor as ourselves.

You've probably noticed that funny things can happen greeting the pastor at the church door.

Sometimes my brain melts after a service and I can call a husband by his wife's name—I've sometimes even done that to some of you! At other times I hear myself say something that is so *apropos* that I don't know where it came from, because I didn't think it up.

Anyway, some time ago, I had done a funeral for an outstanding Christian: a person so faithful and generous and giving and true that my only difficulty was in planning not to say too much and thereby violating his obedience to the word of Jesus about not letting left hand know what the right hand was doing in generous service. So, a celebration of a wonderful Christian life.

At the door, some guy says to me, "I hope someone will speak about me like that, when I go."

I heard my voice saying, "Well, get on with it. What are you waiting for?" The guy gave me one of those looks. But really, what did he expect? We're only going to have good things said at our funeral if there have been good things in our lives to talk about when our life is done. And we will only hear Jesus say, "Well done, good and faithful servant," if we have truly been good and faithful servants.

We're working on this text because it's the gospel for today in the Lectionary. Some of our officers are probably sitting there wondering why I'm not beating the stewardship drum and telling you that our budget is up 13.3% on last year's, and we need you to be faith-full and generous in your support.

In fact, I think I can. I don't mean I want you to buy your way into heaven with a big pledge. It doesn't work like that. But this scripture points us to the lavish generosity of God and the rich blessings we receive—life, family, faith, and all that they lead to—blessings for this life with the promise of richer, more incredible blessings beyond. And how do we respond? Carelessly? Grudgingly? Short-sightedly?

Think of the life of the nation. Tomorrow is Veterans Day. We recall the sacrifice of those who risk their lives and in many cases give their lives in service of the nation. And look at the mess our national response: grubby politics, unscrupulous professionals, self-indulgent excesses, immoral relationships, self-serving conveniences ... The challenges we would overcome with scorn in time of crisis, become insuperable obstacles in the day of small things.

Now think of the church.

- We inherit faith from many who laid down their lives to share it.
- We have more versions of the Bible than ever before.
- We have churches, facilities, provided by the sacrifice of others.
- We have the richest of offerings from the world of music and art to inspire and inform.
- We have the privilege of prayer to bring our concerns before the Lord of heaven.
- We have Jesus— lively enough to silence his critics, and loving enough to secure eternal life through his death and resurrection.

How could we not respond with the best of which we are capable?

You know what it's like in a great marriage. The years bring goals accomplished, and plans fulfilled; trust expands, pleasures deepen, togetherness radiates joy. Sometimes couples finish each other's sentences, sometimes they don't have to. Love at its best.

And love at its best is what God offers us, in this life and the next, if only we would see.

Norman M. Pritchard

Almighty God, you have prepared for those who love you such good things as pass our understanding; pour into our hearts such love toward you that we, loving you above all things, may obtain your promises, which exceed all that we can ask or desire; through Jesus Christ, our Lord. Amen
-The Book of Common Prayer

A Christian to Admire
John 1:35-42

The next day John again was standing with two of his disciples, and as he watched Jesus walk by, he exclaimed, 'Look, here is the Lamb of God!' The two disciples heard him say this, and they followed Jesus. When Jesus turned and saw them following, he said to them, 'What are you looking for?' They said to him, 'Rabbi' (which translated means Teacher), 'where are you staying?' He said to them, 'Come and see.' They came and saw where he was staying, and they remained with him that day. It was about four o'clock in the afternoon. One of the two who heard John speak and followed him was Andrew, Simon Peter's brother. He first found his brother Simon and said to him, 'We have found the Messiah' (which is translated Anointed). He brought Simon to Jesus, who looked at him and said, 'You are Simon son of John. You are to be called Cephas' (which is translated Peter).

Today is the first Sunday of Advent, when the Christian church begins our preparations to celebrate the coming of Jesus. Advent always takes us to the River Jordan and to John the Baptist, whose ministry was to prepare for the coming of Jesus. And in the company of John, we get to see some of his disciples, one of whom was Andrew.

Now, I hope you all know, Andrew is the patron saint of Scotland and today, November 30, is St Andrew's Day and I want to focus on Andrew today, not just because I am an American Scot, but because, also, Andrew has an important Advent perspective to offer.

John's gospel tells us, after meeting Jesus, "The first thing he did was to find his brother Simon and say to him, 'We have found the Messiah.'" Catch the excitement in that: the first thing he did

I sometimes wonder what Simon said in reply to Andrew's excited outburst.

I hope I'm not being unfair to Simon, but I think it's highly possible that he was not impressed. I think Simon probably dismissed Andrew with a comment like, "That's ridiculous, you can't have." I'm guessing, but when you remember Simon's character as revealed in the gospels, I think that is entirely possible. Simon, after all, was the type-A personality, the leader, the initiative taker…

That being so, it would have been Simon's idea that the brothers leave their fishing jobs and travel around 100 miles south to experience for themselves the ministry of John the Baptist, and hear his preaching.

Simon would have been the one most outwardly and openly moved by John's preaching and the amazing sight of crowds streaming for baptism.

And, since Simon's heart always did rule his head, Simon would have suggested that they stay and become John's disciples.

All that would make it strange, now, to hear Andrew claim that he had found the Messiah. Andrew couldn't have found the Messiah! It would surely have been unthinkable, after centuries of Israel's longing for the Messiah, that Andrew, a peasant fisherman, should have been first to find him. No way!

And yet, there was a confidence, an excitement, in the way Andrew spoke that made Simon pause. Andrew was not usually like that. And so, when Andrew repeated his claim, "We have found the Messiah," Simon simply said, "What do you mean?"

It was like opening floodgates. "Remember that man John the Baptist called the Lamb of God? We saw him again yesterday. Two of us met him and stayed to talk with him. We talked all night—about God, about the kingdom of heaven, and about God's plan for his people. Simon, the kingdom of heaven is coming soon, and this man is going to make it happen. The Baptist is right: he's not fit to untie this man's shoes. He's not in the same league. Simon, neither are we. I'm sure he's the Messiah. Come and meet him, Simon. I told him all about you and he wants to meet you …."

And in that simple way, Christian mission is born. Andrew has no sooner caught the germ of the Christian faith, then he spreads it to others: he becomes an enthusiast, an infectious Christian. And in these days, when the world is a mess and the church is under challenge, Andrew is worth our close attention.

I'm struck by Andrew's excitement. The Revised English Bible puts it nicely: "The first thing he did was to find his brother Simon." If you were to read the Greek New Testament at this point, you would notice the breathless style of John's writing—very staccato—reflecting the excitement that overcame Andrew.

But of course! Any piece of good news gets us excited, doesn't it? You call to a friend across the street, or you interrupt a conversation, or you send an e-mail marked urgent, "Bob's past his finals," "Susan's had a baby girl," "They accepted our offer," "Alan is getting married in the new year." Whatever. Good news is news we are excited to share.

Good stores; new cars; the latest cell phone... whatever excites us gets us talking ... great movies.

Joan and I like to go to the movies, but, as you can imagine, I've had one or two things on my plate recently, so Joan was compelled to go see *The Judge* alone. Why did I say 'compelled'? Because a friend who had seen it and loved it kept pushing her: "Have you seen it yet? Want to see it tonight? I'll come with you; I want to see it again."

Several times she phoned, and asked the question, "Have you seen that movie yet?" She went on and on—and on and on—about it, with a kind of missionary zeal. And so, Joan went and saw the film and now she's telling me I need to see it!

Did you notice that I said a "missionary zeal"? Why is it that we can get excited about anything and everything except our faith? Cars, stores, phones, sales, movies can all get us talking enthusiastically to others. But our faith? If good news is news that excites us and demands to be shared, why the silence? Why do we rarely share our faith, and seldom get excited over it?

Now, before you say, that's not my scene, I am a quiet, unobtrusive type of Christian, notice this: so was Andrew. The quieter brother, and in the gospels almost always overshadowed by Simon Peter,

Norman M. Pritchard

Andrew was an unlikely witness. But everyone is. If Christian witness to Jesus required well-qualified Christians, the faith might never have survived.

Christian witness to Jesus does not depend on us: it depends on the Jesus to whom we bear our witness. Andrew's enthusiasm arose because he had found in Jesus the hope that God had not given up on his world, but was faithful to his promises and working to restore his rule. Andrew's nothing special; Jesus is.

And suddenly we see Andrew as an Advent disciple.

Andrew discovers that the longings of centuries, for God to send Messiah have been met,

> That the promises God made have been kept. God has come to visit and redeem his people.

A friend in Michigan recently had to make one of those nightmare journeys to one of his company's branches. Flights at inconvenient times, a long lay-over at some airport and no chance of a return flight the same day. His itinerary was horrible and what made it worse was that he had several urgent matters waiting in his own office.

There was something he had to fix, and as he told me about his awful travel plans, I said: Wouldn't a phone call do instead? Couldn't you do a teleconference or something?

No, he replied; I think this guy is getting seriously out of his depth and I need to look him in the eye and deal with him face to face. Only a face-to-face will do.

As I listened, I thought I detected a Christian parable. Because Jesus is God's face-to-face. Jesus is God's signal that things on earth have gotten seriously out of sync and need a face-to-face.

And that is as true today as it ever was. I'm sure you have felt the mood of anger and hopelessness that fills the air today. Self-serving politicians, business leaders devoid of ethical standards, entertainment shallow and sensational, personal standards slipping;

in many areas an emphasis on style rather than substance and a fog enveloping us that the nation is on the wrong track.

Our world needs a face to face with God. One of my favorite texts is in 2 Corinthians where Paul speaks of "the glory of God in the face of Jesus Christ."[98]

The coming of Jesus brings us face to face with God in his love that redeems a lost world; in his mercy that forgives our shortcomings; in his grace that sustains his people, in his mission that reaches out to others with the good news of God's realm.

No wonder Andrew was excited.

Loving God, fill us with the enthusiasm that gripped Andrew and make us eager to bear glad witness to our faith; that we may show others the hope that Jesus brings and the difference Jesus makes. For your love's sake.

---

[98] 2 Corinthians 4:6.

An Anatomy of Ministry
Luke 3:1-9, 15-17
For an ordination

In the fifteenth year of the reign of Emperor Tiberius, when Pontius Pilate was governor of Judea, and Herod was ruler of Galilee, and his brother Philip ruler of the region of Ituraea and Trachonitis, and Lysanias ruler of Abilene, during the high-priesthood of Annas and Caiaphas, the word of God came to John son of Zechariah in the wilderness. He went into all the region around the Jordan, proclaiming a baptism of repentance for the forgiveness of sins, as it is written in the book of the words of the prophet Isaiah,

> *The voice of one crying out in the wilderness:*
>
> *"Prepare the way of the Lord,*
>
>   *make his paths straight.*
>
> *Every valley shall be filled,*
>
>   *and every mountain and hill shall be made low,*
>
>   *and the crooked shall be made straight,*
>
>   *and the rough ways made smooth;*
>
>   *and all flesh shall see the salvation of God."'*

John said to the crowds that came out to be baptized by him, 'You brood of vipers! Who warned you to flee from the wrath to come? Bear fruits worthy of repentance. Do not begin to say to yourselves, "We have Abraham as our ancestor"; for I tell you, God is able from these stones to raise up children to Abraham. Even now the axe is lying at the root of the trees; every tree therefore that does not bear good fruit is cut down and thrown into the fire.'

... As the people were filled with expectation, and all were questioning in their hearts concerning John, whether he might be the Messiah, John answered all of them by saying, 'I baptize you with water; but one who is more powerful than I is coming; I am not worthy to untie the thong of his sandals. He will baptize you with the Holy Spirit and fire. His winnowing-fork is in his hand, to clear his threshing-floor and to gather the wheat into his granary; but the chaff he will burn with unquenchable fire.'

Stories to Live By

We usually read about John the Baptist in Advent, but I want to suggest him today as a ministry role model, whether we are in full-time ministry, or we are seeking to be faithful in our lives outside the church. If we are going to prepare properly to minister in Christ's name, we're going to have to put our whole selves into it, just as John the Baptist did.

John Baptist is far too modest about his role: 'I am the voice,' he says, 'of one crying in the wilderness, "Make straight the way of the Lord."' (Jn.1:23). John is more than a voice, he is a person; and his whole person, all that he is, is poured into the ministry God has given him.

He is a voice, to be sure, and we'll come to that. But before he used his voice, he used other parts of his anatomy, to serve Christ.

He used his feet. His feet had taken him into the wilderness, away from the routines of daily life into the place where he could be alone and wait on God. Remember the wilderness was where, throughout their history, God's people had been able to come close to God.

So his feet helped him to become a prophet. Of course, there was more to it than that. God had wanted him, prepared him, called him to be a prophet. But John had to use his feet to make it all happen. His feet had taken him to the place where he could hear God properly and know what God was wanting him to do.

Feet are funny like that: they take us places. They express where we are going, in a physical sense, but they also express where we are going metaphorically: they tell us what we are doing. In a sense, feet offer physical indications of who we are and where we're going.

Frederick Buechner advises us,

> If you want to know who you really are, as opposed to who you think you are, keep an eye on where your feet take you.[99]

---

[99] Frederick Buechner, 'Feet' in *Wishful Thinking*. London: Collins,

So, think: where will your feet take you, as you minister in the name of Christ? There's nowhere you will go that he hasn't been before; and nowhere you will go where he will not go with you. Be strong in your trust.

John also used his ears: to hear what God was saying. We take it too readily for granted that John was a prophet. What we need to recall is that John was the first prophet for several hundred years. It was not immediately obvious what message God would want him to deliver, or how he was to deliver it, for the spiritual good of the people. So he used his ears to listen for the word of God.

Before you speak, you must listen, you must learn what to say.

In a world of self-assertion and people pleasing, this is one of the great challenges of Christian ministry. Will Willimon has an interesting article in *The Christian Century*. He'd been to see the movie *The King's Speech* and reflected on the way the king had to be taught to overcome his stammer. He reminded us that pastors have to be taught to overcome their stammering speech.

> Walking naked down Main Street while playing a harmonica is nothing compared to the personal exposure required to talk about God for 20 minutes to a group of people who have been, all week long, avoiding even the merest mention of God.
>
> Few of us preachers mount a pulpit on Sunday morning because we are truly good at it and enjoy mouthing off before a crowd. We got put there.[100]

So trust the God who put you here.

Then John uses his finger: he points. John's most important ministry is to point to Christ: Behold the lamb of God who takes away the sin of the world. It was an extraordinary ministry, to tell people, who were confident that they belonged to God, that they needed to be

---

[100] William Willimon, "Voice Lessons" *The Christian Century*, February 8, 2011, 10-12.

cleansed and baptized, to receive the forgiveness that God would make available through the death of his Son, the Lamb of God.

He pointed out that people need to change; that human lives and lifestyles alienate us from God and from each other; and that God sends his Son into the world, for just that purpose. Not a popular role, to point to Christ like that, especially to point people to Christ who were satisfied that God approved of them as they were.

The modern equivalent to the attitude of people in John's day is the way people today assume that their belonging to the church is all it takes to please God.

It's a danger always before us: to be so smug about the church that we point to the church, to ourselves, rather than to Christ.

Peter Gomes of Harvard has a great story of a time he preached at St Giles' in Edinburgh. Gilleasbuig MacMillan, the minister there, warned him before the service that the good folk of Edinburgh were unlikely to be friendly or cordial. 'It's not like your American churches,' he said, 'they don't say anything, but don't take it personally.' Gomes recalls,

> So I preached as well as God enabled me, and after the service, at the door of St Giles, he was right: not a word of greeting or welcome as these dour Presbyterians passed by, until one lady took my hand, and looked me straight in the eye and said, 'Ah, it must have been a great honor for you to preach to us this morning.'[101]

She was right, but for the wrong reason. It was not an honor because of who she was, or her fellow congregants; it was an honor, a privilege, because God uses humble servants such as us to point to Christ and set him loose to help or heal, to bless or distress, and so to bring God right to the very center of the human heart. Too bad the woman missed that.

Which brings us to the topic of his voice: for what John has heard, and is pointing to, he must proclaim. What God has told him, he

---

[101] Peter Gomes, can't find the reference in one of his books.

must tell the world. 'Among you stands one whom you do not know; the one who is coming after me; I am not worthy to untie the thong of his sandal .... Behold the lamb of God,' he said

The former French president Francois Mitterand was once asked what quality is necessary in a great leader. He said, "Well, I'd like to say 'sincerity', but I'm afraid I must say 'indifference'. Gore Vidal interpreted this statement to mean

> You bring yourself to the point of indifference so that you can examine a situation with as little emotion and as much logic and intelligence as you can bring to it, which you cannot bring to it if your heart is breaking.[102]

That may be leadership; it's not Christian leadership. It's not the servant leadership of Christ. Our Christ is the very opposite of that: instead of indifference he brought involvement, involvement expressed as costly sacrificial love.

- To a world of lostness and despair, he brought the light of God's truth;

- to a world of sin and confusion, he brought forgiveness and grace;

- to a world of hurt and loss, he brought the peace of God's presence;

- to your world and mine, he brought God's blessing and God's love, where we most need them now.

That's the pattern of our ministry: we teach, we preach, not because we need to get something off our chests but because we want to get something out of our hearts—the love God put there and calls us to share extravagantly with God's people.

---

[102] Gore Vidal *New York Times* interview, syndicated to *The Age* Good Weekend November 25, 1995, 31.

A Procession of Thoughts
Psalm 118:15-29

There are glad songs of victory in the tents of the righteous:
'The right hand of the Lord does valiantly;
* the right hand of the Lord is exalted;*
* the right hand of the Lord does valiantly.'*
I shall not die, but I shall live,
* and recount the deeds of the Lord.*
The Lord has punished me severely,
* but he did not give me over to death.*
Open to me the gates of righteousness,
* that I may enter through them*
* and give thanks to the Lord.*

This is the gate of the Lord;
* the righteous shall enter through it.*
I thank you that you have answered me
* and have become my salvation.*
The stone that the builders rejected
* has become the chief cornerstone.*
This is the Lord's doing;
* it is marvelous in our eyes.*
This is the day that the Lord has made;
* let us rejoice and be glad in it.*

Norman M. Pritchard

Save us, we beseech you, O Lord!

*   O Lord, we beseech you, give us success!*

Blessed is the one who comes in the name of the Lord.

*   We bless you from the house of the Lord.*

The Lord is God,

*   and he has given us light.*

Bind the festal procession with branches,

*   up to the horns of the altar.*

You are my God, and I will give thanks to you;

*   you are my God, I will extol you.*

O give thanks to the Lord, for he is good,

*   for his steadfast love endures forever.*

There's nothing better than singing hymns we know and love. They may have special associations in our minds that make them precious to us, or they may just be familiar, and we know the tune and love to sing them.

Sometimes the familiarity pulls up the memories we associate with the hymn.: the church we grew up in, our summer church up north, a family wedding or memorial service. These memories flood our minds and bless us every time we sing the hymn.

Sometimes, though, sheer familiarity tempts our minds to wander and our thoughts to drift. We're singing the words, but we're thinking about what's happening at work, the argument we had in the car on the way to church, Sunday brunch—whatever. The meaning is lost because our minds are miles away.

You know how that can happen ....? I know it happens during sermons, but right now we're thinking about hymns. It can happen when we're singing hymns!

Well, go back to that first Palm Sunday and listen to the pilgrims singing Psalm 118. They always sing it on the way to Jerusalem for festivals like Passover.

> *Open to me the gates of righteousness,*
>
> *that I may enter through them and give thanks to the Lord.*
>
> *This is the gate of the Lord, the righteous shall enter through it...*
>
> *The stone that the builders rejected has become the chief cornerstone*
>
> *This is the Lord's doing, it is marvelous in our eyes...*
>
> *(Hosanna!) Save us, we beseech you, O Lord!*
>
> *O Lord, we beseech you, give us success!*

All Jews love that psalm. It celebrates God's past deliverance and expresses longing that God will once again deliver them. Soon, they hope. But the words are familiar, maybe too familiar for some. What if the disciples sing the words but let their minds go wandering off to other thoughts ...?

Peter is puzzled and perplexed.

Hosanna means 'Save now.'

The people are giving the psalm an extra meaning: They spread cloaks before Jesus as they would welcome a king. They wave palms as a sign of God's victory. It is as though the people are hailing Jesus as the Messiah who will drive out the Romans, and Jesus does not seem to mind. Yet when he had called Jesus Messiah, Jesus had rejected the suggestion, and with violent language: Get behind me Satan, he had said.

Peter is thinking that he doesn't really understand Jesus too well. What's happening doesn't seem to make much sense. So, Peter is puzzled as he sings. He doesn't understand.

Unlike his brother, Andrew is happy.

From his first meeting with Jesus, Andrew has loved Jesus and has been keen to introduce people to him. So Andrew is pleased to see

Jesus with a crowd. As long as people are meeting Jesus, listening to Jesus, learning about God from Jesus, Andrew's happy.

He watches the crowd of pilgrims sing "Blessed is he who comes in the name of the Lord". Well, that's great, he thinks, Jesus comes in the name of the Lord. The people are celebrating his Jesus, acknowledging his Master. Andrew thinks of all the good that Jesus can do for these people, and he's glad.

His fishing partner, James, son of Zebedee, has quite a different thought in mind. He likes to see Jesus in the limelight like this too, because some of the limelight might reflect on his disciples

These pilgrims come from Galilee, perhaps some from Capernaum. If they see him at Jesus' side, it will be great publicity. "One of Jesus' right hand men" is a valuable testimonial. Good for business. In years to come people will remember that and think, Zebedee and Sons have connections with Jesus: they must be an honest firm, we'll do business with them. So, James jostles in the crowd, to get a more prominent position.

His brother John is thinking deeper thoughts. He loves Jesus and tries very hard to understand him. He knows the kingdom Jesus speaks about is not of this world. He recalls that time when Jesus was transfigured, and God acknowledged Jesus. God is with Jesus, that much is clear. God is going to do something very special through Jesus. But then, why did Jesus arrange for this parade? Jesus doesn't need the crowds from Galilee if God is with him. Does he?

Thomas too, is thinking about the crowds. He's worried things might just get out of hand. Jesus has enemies, and too big a demonstration might provoke the authorities into breaking up the procession and making examples of one or two leaders.

A week ago, he'd tried to warn Jesus not to come to Judaea because the Jews would try to stone him. Jesus seemed determined, so Thomas had said, "Let us go and die with him." Brave words—and he meant them. Then. Only now he's not so sure. He doesn't like the thought of dying, but he's not sure he can escape. He hears the words he's singing "I shall not die but live" and he thinks Oh,

God, I hope that's right. "Lord deliver us we pray." These verses sum up all his thoughts.

Thaddeus is there, as he always is and, as he always is, he's very hard to read. I mean, did you remember that he is numbered among the 12? Exactly. That's the way he was, there but uninvolved. He never seems to have said anything or done anything. A disciple who did nothing! Makes you wonder why our Lord even called him ...

Philip wonders what Jesus is up to. You see, when arrangements have to be made, Phillip usually makes them. Like when Jesus wanted the crowds fed, Jesus turned to him—arrangements and details were his strong point. This time Jesus had already made arrangements for the donkey—all he did was go to Bethany with Andrew and pick it up. And, so far as he knew, nothing had been planned for Passover. Yet Jesus knew Jerusalem would be crowded, and they couldn't rent a room at the last moment—so what was he doing? Had Jesus made arrangements without involving him, and if so why? Curious.

Nathanael leaves all arrangements to others. He is singing the psalm with faith and joy. He loves the Passover season and its entire religious associations: the festival, the Temple sacrifice, the feast, remembering the Exodus and God's mighty acts of deliverance and salvation. This is religion at its best, its most moving.

The excitement mounts as the procession moves along and he briefly wonders how many of the people really understand—or care. These days too many people only want the holiday, not the religion. But Nathanael won't let that dampen his excitement or his faith: he loves Passover!

Simon is excited, but for a very different reason. All his adult life he has waited for this, for God to send the Messiah to overthrow the hated Romans and restore the kingdom to Israel. He joined the Zealots. People call him Simon the Zealot. A freedom fighter! A God's kingdom fighter! He suspects that Jesus has his plans most carefully made. He thinks Jesus is right not to reveal them too soon. Careless talk costs lives. He wonders where they'll get their weapons?

James son of Alphaeus has Zealot sympathies too, although not everybody knows that. He's a bit worried about the crowd, today. They seem just ordinary people going to Jerusalem for the Passover. Oh, they want rid of the Romans all right, but will they do anything to help? They're devoted to their nation and loyal to their religion—provided someone else does all the work and takes the risks. And people can be very fickle: with you all the way one moment, but liable to abandon you if you look like losing. James hopes Jesus has better support than this lot.

Jude is watching the crowd also—but he is worrying about an attack. He's heard the word on the street that Barabbas has something planned this Passover. Jude knows that if Barabbas thought Jesus might be making a rival move, he would try to destroy it before it damaged his own efforts. And everybody knows you don't mix with Barabbas if you're smart. So, Jude thinks it's a wise move to keep an eye out for trouble and he scans the crowd with darting, anxious eyes.

Judas Iscariot is appalled by what he sees. He can't believe that Jesus lets this happen. The crowd treats Jesus as some kind of Messiah, but one look tells you that there's no way they are going to manage a revolt. It's suicide. He'll be killed, and he'll take all those people with him. The Romans will cut them to shreds. Well (he thinks) if Jesus wants to commit suicide that's his business. I don't, and I won't. Just then a thought with worrying implications creeps into his mind: Jesus must be stopped!   It is better that one man should die for the people than that the nation be destroyed.

A procession of thoughts and a confusion of thoughts.

And in the center of this mixed-up moment, sits Jesus:

On the donkey he had chosen as the sign of peace, not war.

- At Passover time when lambs are sacrificed to recall God's love for his people.

- He is tense with the thought of the approaching ordeal.

- He is sad that the people's hearts are so confused.

- And he thinks of the death he knows he will die
for the nation, and not for the nation alone but to gather
together all the scattered children of God.

And he sings the psalm,

> *I shall not die, I shall live to proclaim what the Lord has done*
>
> *The Lord did indeed chasten me, but he did not surrender me to death...*
>
> *The stone which the builders have rejected has become the head of the corner.*
>
> *This is the Lord's doing, it is wonderful in his eyes...*
>
> *It is good to give thanks to the Lord, for his love endures forever.*

Sort out our thoughts, dear Lord, and clear our minds,
that as we follow you on the way to the cross,
we may see your redeeming purpose and believe your redeeming love,
and in response live our lives as faithful followers in your way.
We ask it in your name, Amen.

Remember What Your Mother Told You
Acts 16:16-30

One day, as we were going to the place of prayer, we met a slave-girl who had a spirit of divination and brought her owners a great deal of money by fortune-telling. While she followed Paul and us, she would cry out, 'These men are slaves of the Most High God, who proclaim to you a way of salvation.' She kept doing this for many days. But Paul, very much annoyed, turned and said to the spirit, 'I order you in the name of Jesus Christ to come out of her.' And it came out that very hour.

But when her owners saw that their hope of making money was gone, they seized Paul and Silas and dragged them into the market-place before the authorities. When they had brought them before the magistrates, they said, 'These men are disturbing our city; they are Jews and are advocating customs that are not lawful for us as Romans to adopt or observe.' The crowd joined in attacking them, and the magistrates had them stripped of their clothing and ordered them to be beaten with rods. After they had given them a severe flogging, they threw them into prison and ordered the jailer to keep them securely. Following these instructions, he put them in the innermost cell and fastened their feet in the stocks.

About midnight Paul and Silas were praying and singing hymns to God, and the prisoners were listening to them. Suddenly there was an earthquake, so violent that the foundations of the prison were shaken; and immediately all the doors were opened and everyone's chains were unfastened. When the jailer woke up and saw the prison doors wide open, he drew his sword and was about to kill himself, since he supposed that the prisoners had escaped. But Paul shouted in a loud voice, 'Do not harm yourself, for we are all here.' The jailer called for lights, and rushing in, he fell down trembling before Paul and Silas. Then he brought them outside and said, 'Sirs, what must I do to be saved?'

Happy Mother's Day to all moms in the congregation and good memories to every child of a mother in the congregation. (I think that's all of you!)

It's nice to think that the ideal behind Mother's Day still exists—happy families, good relationships, love and warmth and security. And we need to pray for families to experience those precious gifts.

Even so, it's also important to resist the Mother's Day mush and acknowledge that we are fallible creatures and even relationships at home must struggle with disappointment. Alyce McKenzie is a New Testament theologian in Dallas and she wrote about a phone call she once received from her mom.

> "This Mother's Day, please don't send me another card covered with flowers and filled with flattery. I appreciate your thinking of me, but they always make me cry."
>
> "Why is that, Mom?"
>
> "Oh, Come on, Alyce. Get real! I did the best I could, but I was far from a perfect mom! You remember. You were there!"
>
> So this year I got her a card with that old woman on it with the hairnet and the housedress with a ciggie hanging out of her lip. On the front it says, "Hours of excruciating labor. Millions of poopie diapers. Countless sleepless nights."
>
> ... inside it says, "And you get a card . . . Yeah, that sounds fair."[103]

Poor Mom! It often is unfair. I mean, mom's the principle teacher in the home, right? But we don't always appreciate that role, as this story demonstrates. Here's a story I dedicate to my wife and mother of our children:

A nine-year-old pipes up from the back seat of the car, "Mommy, who told Daddy how to drive before he married you?"!! And I can almost hear Joan retort, "Whoever it was, didn't do a very good job!!

---

[103] Alyce McKenzie, "'M' is for the Many Things: A Sermon for Mother's Day." Patheos: Edgy Exegesis.
http://www.patheos.com//Progressive-Christian/M-is-for-the-Many-Things-Alyce-McKenzie-05-08-2013.html

So, despite our failings, Mother's Day allows us to affirm a special relationship, a profound dependence and, hopefully gifts that we can carry with us through our life. Among those gifts are the things your mother told you that you'll always remember. Like—

- Always wear clean underwear—in case you're in an accident.
- Always say your prayers at night before you go to bed.
- And—a favorite of my mom's—if a thing's worth doing, it's worth doing well.

I wonder if St Paul had a mom? That's a silly way to put it—of course he had a mom. Only he never mentions her. When he talks about his past and his pride in his upbringing, he never mentions mom. He writes to Timothy and celebrates Timothy's mother and grandmother, but never mentions his own.

Doesn't really matter. Moms are moms the world over. They feel the same love; face the same challenges; they say the same things. I think Paul would be glad to have received from his mom the advice we got from ours.

Always wear clean underwear in case you're in an accident. I wonder if Paul thought of that advice, when he was in Philippi, on the day when the owners of the slave girl got so ticked off because Paul had cured their money-machine that they started a demonstration and the demonstration ended with the magistrates stripping Paul and Silas of their clothing and flogging them.[104]

The issue, of course, is not underwear; the issue is the unexpected. Be ready for the unexpected. Mom told us that! We will not always be in control of our lives, and things will happen that we did not plan and, often, do not want—but still we'll have to deal with them. Be ready!

I've shared these words with you before, but they bear repeating. They're the wonderful honesty with which Barbara Brown Taylor faces the unexpected she encountered in her life:

---

[104] Acts 16:22.

> I have set out to be married and ended up divorced. I have set out to be healthy and ended up sick. I have set out to live in New England and ended up in Georgia. When I was thirty, I set out to be a parish priest … Almost 13 years later, I teach school….[105]

Mom told us—be ready for the unexpected.

So unexpectedly, the thanks that Paul and Silas get for healing a poor slave girl is that they are stripped and flogged and thrown into prison. And then we see that Paul remembered another gem from mother: say your prayers at night before you go to sleep. Verse 25: About midnight Paul and Silas were praying and singing hymns to God.

Perhaps, like Stephen earlier in Acts, they are rejoicing that they are sharing in the suffering of Christ at the hands of an unbelieving world.

Perhaps like Bonhoeffer, they're confused to find themselves in prison and wonder what it says about them. Bonhoeffer cut an impressive figure to others, but inside he was uncertain and perplexed. He wrote a poem that is also a prayer. It ends in faith:

> Who am I? They mock me those lonely questions of mine.
> Whoever I am, thou knowest, O Lord, I am thine.[106]

Perhaps Paul And Silas prayed like that. Or, perhaps, like Jesus in Gethsemane, they pray for release but add, "Nevertheless not my will, but yours be done," a prayer of trust and surrender that commits the outcome to God.

Prayer does that for us and to us. Peace; security; assurance. "My times are in your hand." Remember what your mother told you—say your prayers at night.

---

[105] Barbara Brown Taylor, *An Altar in the World. A Geography of Faith.* New York: HarperCollins, 2009, 72-73.
[106] Dietrich Bonhoeffer, *Letters and Papers From Prison.* ET Glasgow: Fontana Books, 8th impression 1966, 173.

And then, the earthquake. The apostles were new in Philippi. They did not know the town was prone to earthquakes. But it must have seemed a miracle, a chance to escape and enjoy a private vindication. They didn't take it. If a thing's worth doing, my mom always told me, it's worth doing well.

Paul and Silas were engaged in Christian mission and a cheap escape would have poisoned the well for the church in Philippi. They didn't run. Instead they chose the way of faithfulness, integrity, courage and commitment. They chose to face their opposition, not run away and hide.

When trouble strikes, our weaker nature wants a miracle. We want a way out. "Dear Lord, bend the rules for me. Just a little miracle please. I'm in a tight spot."

In all our challenges, what God offers us is a way through, not a way out. What God wants in us is not weakness but strength, not cowardice that runs but courage that stands and stays, and what God wants, God also offers, as Bonhoeffer wrote from prison:

> Christ not only makes [people] 'good;' he makes them strong too....[107]

...echoing the truth Paul later shared with the Philippians, I can do all things through him who strengthens me.[108]

That verse often features in missives that make their way round the Internet, along the lines "God has not promised'. In his latest book, Adam Hamilton tells of Annie Johnson Flint whose life was marked by a catalog of misfortune and suffering. But he notes,

> Annie is perhaps best remembered for a poem she wrote called "What God Hath Promised":
>
> God hath not promised skies always blue,
> Flower strewn pathways all our lives through;
> God hath not promised sun without rain,

---

[107] Bonhoeffer, *Letters* Abridged Edition, London: SCM Press,1981, 143.
[108] Philippians 4:13.

Joy without sorrow, peace without pain.

But God hath promised strength for the day,
Rest for the labor, light for the way,
Grace for the trials, help from above,
Unfailing sympathy, undying love.[109]

Some of the things our mothers told us resonate so closely with Christian teaching that I think it's appropriate to acknowledge Mother's Day in church. We're not pretending mom was perfect, but we recognize reflections of the love of God in motherhood at its best.

Mother's love may be imperfect, but it has moments of unconditional love within it.

So: remember what your mother told you. Use it as a pointer to the love of God that never changes, and never gives us up.

For the love in which we were created and the love in which we are sustained and the love which never gives us up, Lord, we give you thanks and praise, in Jesus' name.

---

[109] Adam Hamilton, *Half Truths, God Helps Those Who Help Themselves and Other Things the Bible Doesn't Say.* Nashville, TN: Abingdon Press, 2016, 101

An Almost Unsung Hero
Philippians 2:19-30

Commencement for Pittsburgh Theological Seminary, 2007

I hope in the Lord Jesus to send Timothy to you soon, so that I may be cheered by news of you. I have no one like him who will be genuinely concerned for your welfare. All of them are seeking their own interests, not those of Jesus Christ. But Timothy's worth you know, how like a son with a father he has served with me in the work of the gospel. I hope therefore to send him as soon as I see how things go with me; and I trust in the Lord that I will also come soon.

Still, I think it necessary to send to you Epaphroditus—my brother and co-worker and fellow-soldier, your messenger and minister to my need; for he has been longing for all of you, and has been distressed because you heard that he was ill. He was indeed so ill that he nearly died. But God had mercy on him, and not only on him but on me also, so that I would not have one sorrow after another. I am the more eager to send him, therefore, in order that you may rejoice at seeing him again, and that I may be less anxious. Welcome him then in the Lord with all joy, and honor such people, because he came close to death for the work of Christ, risking his life to make up for those services that you could not give me.

Class of 2007—warm congratulations! You have this ceremony to go through and then you're finished with school and out into God's world. For some of you, the first steps in ministry beckon; others return to ministry refocused and renewed. May God bless you and go with you!

You hardly need me to tell you, you are going into a crazy world; a world where we wish Andy Warhol had been right about people getting 15 minutes of fame. We wish Anna Nicole and Paris and Angelina, and all the rest *only got* 15 minutes, and no more!

We read tonight of someone who almost missed his 15 minutes. No, not Timothy, Epaphroditus.

If he had not fallen sick while ministering to Paul, we might never have heard of him. His illness gave Paul occasion to mention him and gave us the chance to appreciate his ministry.

Stories to Live By

Paul speaks of "our brother Epaphroditus, my fellow-worker and fellow-soldier, your messenger and minister to my need."

Now, if you had been members of the First Presbyterian Church of Dallas[110], you'd have been following our reading in your Greek New Testaments, and you'd have noticed that Paul uses five words to commend Epaphroditus. They are five great, descriptive words that I want to offer you tonight as aspirations for your ministry.

Brother. You know, of course, how remarkable it is that Paul, the former Pharisee, should use the word 'brother' of someone whose name evokes the cult of the pagan goddess of sex and fertility. But that's Christianity for you: it breaks down barriers and gives us sisters and brothers in unexpected people.

That opens up wonderful vistas of privilege and responsibility. We get to stand with people at the great moments of their lives—the great wonderful moments and the great terrible moments, and we're there because of the grace and love of God. But because of what we do, sometimes people see us as just a little different, perhaps even special; they think our calling sets us, somehow, apart. Don't let that happen—and be warned, it can happen to the best of us!

It was only when she left the parish after 15 years of incredibly effective ministry, that Barbara Brown Taylor saw how disconnected she'd become. The clerical collar she had worn six days a week, she discovered, had set her apart as surely "as a velvet rope in a museum."[111]

> ... people treated me like the Virgin Mary's younger sister. They watched their language. They shielded me from their darker natures. They guarded my purity.[112]

She decided it was time to change. She announced her resignation to her congregation and prepared to depart. Soon thereafter, a couple

---

[110] An affectionate salute to the seminary President, Dr Bill Cail, who regularly taught New Testament Greek classes to his congregation in First Presbyterian Church, Dallas TX.
[111] Barbara Brown Taylor, *Leaving Church A Memoir of Faith*. San Francisco: HarperSanFrancisco, 2006, 144.
[112] Taylor, *Leaving*, 145.

of church members invited her to their pool party—a legendary event in the town's social calendar: live Maine lobsters and kegs of imported beer. Glad to be included, Taylor accepted.

She enjoyed chatting with people—real conversations now, not church talk. She watched the children splashing in the floodlit pool. Suddenly, with noisy hilarity, someone threw a fully clothed adult into the pool. Mayhem ensued as people tried to throw others in and they resisted. Several made for Taylor, but stopped in their tracks: she was, after all, a pastor. But eventually someone grabbed her from behind and threw her in. She recalls,

> I never found out who my savior was, but when I broke the surface, I looked around at all those shining people with makeup running down their cheeks, with hair plastered to their heads, and I was so happy to be one of them.... Bobbing in that healing pool with all those other flawed beings of light, I looked around and saw them as I had never seen them before, while some of them looked at me the same way. The long wait had come to an end. I was in the water at last.[113]

The echoes of baptism in that story are frightening, as is the way—I'm sure you noticed—she describes the joker who threw her in: "my savior." She needed saving from her role, to feel connected to the people. In the name of the Jesus who laid aside his glory for incarnational ministry, don't make that mistake.

Remember your theology of ministry. Be human: serve as sister, brother.

Then Paul calls Epaphroditus his fellow-worker.

'Fellow worker' describes those who work with Paul to spread the gospel, and what could be more fulfilling than that? Nothing! When we hear God's call—to whatever Christian ministry—there's something in us hoping for a vocation like Moses' or Jeremiah's or Paul's: a high and holy calling to do great things for God.

---

[113] Taylor, *Leaving*, 118-20.

But what happens? Often, we spend our evenings weighing competing bids for a carpet in the nursery, or finding someone—anyone! —to chaperone the youth mission trip. Tasks so mundane that we need God's Spirit to do them faithfully! Sometimes we get to set out chairs for a meeting.

Gordon Atkinson does that. For 16 years he's been pastor of a church worshipping in rented accommodation, so chairs were set out and put away at every service. He did it. He says you go through stages.

Excitement—the shortest stage. It only lasts about halfway through your first Sunday.

Resignation—the "Whatever. Someone's gotta do it" stage.

Boredom follows, then acceptance. Pride is next: "No one can set up chairs like you. Not faster. Not better." But eventually a sixth stage sets in—

> Love—this last stage comes after carrying out any menial task for your faith community over many years. You begin to see small things as big things and vice versa. Setting up chairs is like offering a cup of cold water in the name of Christ. It's a small part of the kingdom, but it is your part. It's been so long since anyone else in the church set up chairs that some people don't even know how it gets done…

I've been in stage six, the love stage, for about five years now…

> Setting up chairs has become a prayer. It is speaking in tongues. It is my own secret prayer language, offered to the heavens in those wonderful moments when no one is at the church but me.[114]

So live a theology of service. Be faithful—love your work.

---

[114] Gordon Atkinson, "Chairs and Prayers" Real Live Preacher, December 26, 2006.
http://www.christiancentury.org/article.lasso?id=2803

Paul also calls Epaphroditus his 'fellow-soldier.' Soldier? Yes: we're in a fight today—a fight for truth and faith and love.

Bad enough that you have to fight the likes of Sam Harris and Richard Dawkins and their hostility to the faith; but sometimes the battle's nearer home than that. In a recent *Christian Century*, John Buchanan tells of keeping up with what people are reading. He picked up Joel Osteen's *Your Best Life Now*.

> "Enlarge your vision," [Osteen writes]. "If you develop an image of victory, success, health, abundance, joy, peace and happiness, nothing on earth will be able to hold those things from you. . . . God wants to increase you financially, by giving you promotions, fresh ideas, creativity." [John comments] As I read, I kept thinking about the people I know who face challenges that do not and will not respond to an "enlarged vision." [115]

Buchanan says, he put the book down. I don't mean to boast, but I went one better: I returned my copy to the bookstore and got my money back! I didn't want to encourage the book's sales figures!

When the greed and self-fixation of our culture are offered—and eagerly accepted—as Christianity, we Christians have a fight on our hands!

So develop your apologetics. Be truthful—defend the faith.

Then Paul calls Epaphroditus 'messenger.' You've noticed, since you're following in the Greek, that Paul actually used the word 'apostle' at this point. An apostle was simply a messenger who was sent. "As the Father has sent me, so I send you… Receive the Holy Spirit," Jesus told the disciples in John 20.

All ministry is missional. So I hope that, wherever your ministry takes you, you will remember that the Son has sent you on the Father's mission in the Spirit's power. Let the cross-cultural mission experiences the seminary had given you inspire you for that other,

---

[115] John M. Buchanan, "Read and Unread "The *Christian Century*, May 01, 2007, 3

difficult mission you will engage in: the one at your front door. God is at work in the world! Faith is flourishing!

Thanks to the seminary's World Mission Initiative, my congregation is developing sister-church relationships with Central Baptist Church in Moscow. I know we'll receive far more than we'll ever give. The story of how the faith survived the communist onslaught is inspiring.

Communism has been replaced by Vladimir Putin's inscrutable policies and Christians are still wary. Central Baptist doesn't maintain a membership roll—they can't be confident the state won't turn against them again and use the membership list as a hit list for harassment and persecution... It makes me wonder, how many church members would *we* have, in such circumstances?

For decades, most Russian Christians only possessed small portions of the bible, if they'd been able to copy them out by hand, from hand-written copies of hand-written copies, stretching back who knows how far! In the West, where we have a bewildering variety of customized bibles for every conceivable market niche, we don't even bother now to carry our bibles to church!

I am profoundly challenged by a comment Michael Bordeaux of Keston College made about Russian Christianity,

> Usually Christianity does not need to evangelize: it just needs to be itself.[116]

That is not a recipe for lazy Christianity, for sitting back complacently. It's a challenge to be so living in the love of Christ that Jesus is able to work through us the things we learn he's doing in other parts of the world. It is a challenge to stir ourselves to catch up with what God's doing in the world! Scott Sunquist cites Harold Kurtz, "The Gospel is out of control."[117] Take courage!

---

[116] Michael Bourdeaux, *Risen Indeed Lessons in Faith from the USSR*. London: Darton, Longman and Todd, 1983, 98.
[117] Harold Kurtz, cited in W Scott Sunquist, "Presbyterian Mission in a Flat World." Address to the New Wilmington Missionary Conference, 26 July 2006.

Draw strength from your theology of mission. Be fruitful—spread the faith

Then Paul calls Epaphroditus 'minister to my need.' He uses Greek word *leitourgos*, which gives us English words like 'liturgy.'

Liturgy was originally any piece of service, often public service, people undertook. Then it came to mean that special work that people do, which is the worship of God. That makes for a special challenge for those of you who'll spend time leading worship—to make worship real enough to connect the work your people do in the world, with the work we do together in worship.

And in the world of Enron, WorldCom and executives on massive salaries while workers lose their jobs, that means the Christian claims of love and justice need emphasizing and Christian values in the workplace need encouraging. It doesn't always happen.

Princeton theologian Ellen Charry can quip, apropos today's disconnect between faith and work:

> The laity that populates the corporate world is pressed to either close their ears in church or hold their noses at work.[118]

Since faith involves encounter with the living God who seeks to meet with us in worship, yes, but also in the world, our challenge is to worship in ways that enable that encounter. Our worship is too often routine.

When George MacLeod was setting up the Iona Community in Scotland, a major row broke out between two members. MacLeod recalls,

> Someone suggested a special prayer meeting about it. When I pointed out that we already had worship in the Abbey each morning and evening, someone said, "Oh, yes, that's just

---

[118] Ellen Charry, "Am I My Brother's Keeper?" in *Theology Today*, October 2003, 294.

ordinary divine worship," implying that no one expected much to happen in ordinary divine worship.[119]

If worship has not changed us, it has not been worship. If worship does not relate church on Sunday to what happens Monday, it has not been worship.

Perfect your theology of worship. Be worshipful; and live the faith.

Just one thing more. Speaking of Epaphroditus, Paul tells the church at Philippi,

> Welcome him then in the Lord with all joy, and honor such people.

Such people? So there were more than one of him? Of course, there were! And are! They are here tonight, the class of 2007: signs that God has not given up on his world yet because he has not given up on his church yet:

God calls to ministry and service;

> God inspires with truth and faith;

>> God empowers with Spirit not of our arranging.

Joy is a fitting response. Joy in the Lord is our strength.

And now, to him who by the power at work within us is able to accomplish abundantly far more than we can ask or imagine, to him be glory in the church and in Christ Jesus to all generations, forever and ever. Amen

---

[119] Ron Ferguson, *George MacLeod*. London: Collins, 1990, 161.

The Dove—Our Assurance
Genesis 8:6-22

Part of a series of sermons on the seal of the Presbyterian Church (USA) and the elements of the Christian faith that they illustrate.

In Memory of those who lost their lives in Las Vegas, October 1, 2017

At the end of forty days Noah opened the window of the ark that he had made and sent out the raven; and it went to and fro until the waters were dried up from the earth. Then he sent out the dove from him, to see if the waters had subsided from the face of the ground; but the dove found no place to set its foot, and it returned to him to the ark, for the waters were still on the face of the whole earth. So he put out his hand and took it and brought it into the ark with him. He waited another seven days, and again he sent out the dove from the ark; and the dove came back to him in the evening, and there in its beak was a freshly plucked olive leaf; so Noah knew that the waters had subsided from the earth. Then he waited another seven days, and sent out the dove; and it did not return to him anymore.

In the six hundred first year, in the first month, the first day of the month, the waters were dried up from the earth; and Noah removed the covering of the ark, and looked, and saw that the face of the ground was drying. In the second month, on the twenty-seventh day of the month, the earth was dry.

Then God said to Noah, "Go out of the ark, you and your wife, and your sons and your sons' wives with you. Bring out with you every living thing that is with you of all flesh—birds and animals and every creeping thing that creeps on the earth—so that they may abound on the earth, and be fruitful and multiply on the earth." So Noah went out with his sons and his wife and his sons' wives. And every animal, every creeping thing, and every bird, everything that moves on the earth, went out of the ark by families.

Then Noah built an altar to the LORD, *and took of every clean animal and of every clean bird, and offered burnt offerings on the altar. And when the* LORD *smelled the pleasing odor, the* LORD *said in his heart, "I will never again curse the ground because of humankind, for the inclination of the human heart is evil from youth; nor will I ever again destroy every living creature as I have done. As long as the earth endures, seedtime and harvest, cold and heat, summer and winter, day and night, shall not cease."*

An interesting anniversary fell last Monday, October 2. On that date in 1950, Charles M Shultz's *Peanuts* cartoon series made its debut.[120] The first strip shows a boy and a girl, sitting on a sidewalk. The boy, Shermy, says, "Well! Here comes ol' Charlie Brown! Good ol' Charlie Brown ... Yes, sir! Good ol' Charlie Brown." After Charlie Brown walks away, Shermy adds, "How I hate him!" In the second Peanuts strip the girl, Patty, walks alone, chanting, "Little girls are made of sugar and spice ... and everything nice." As Charlie Brown comes up to her, she slugs him and says, "That's what little girls are made of!"

The strip offered many illustrations of its central themes:

> People, especially children, are selfish and cruel to one another; social life is perpetual conflict; one's deepest wishes will invariably be derailed and one's comforts whisked away...

Shultz made us face the brokenness of life, the evil that lurks in the human heart. Was it despite that, or because of that, that *Peanuts* became an amazing success: carried by more than 2,600 newspapers all over the world? One scholar of popular culture called it "arguably the longest story told by a single artist in human history."

The longest-running story in human history is the story, told by hundreds, of the flood.

> The ancient world was full of flood stories. A researcher named John D. Morris collected more than 200 of them, from ancient China, India, Native American cultures and beyond. He calculates that in 88 percent of the tales there is a favored family. In 70 percent, they survive the flood in a boat. In 67 percent, the animals are also saved in the boat.

---

[120] Sarah Boxer, "The Exemplary Narcissism of Snoopy," *The Atlantic* November 2015. Accessed at https://www.theatlantic.com/magazine/archive/2015/11/the-exemplary-narcissism-of-snoopy/407827/?utm_source=nl-atlantic-daily-100217&silverid=MzEwMTkwMTU3Nzg5S0

> In 66 percent, the flood is due to the wickedness of man, and in 57 percent the boat comes to rest on a mountain top.[121]

These stories—including the Genesis one—represent an attempt to interpret the memory of some catastrophic flood at some early point in history. It's interesting that two thirds of them start from the premise of human wickedness, and although the story presents a very primitive picture of God, the truth the narrative explores is the truth of both the judgment of God and the grace of God.

The flood story affirms that there is such a thing as divine judgment. Not a popular topic, to be sure. These days no one wants to think about judgment. In all the opinion polls, far more Americans say they believe in heaven than say they believe in hell. But in these days of horror and suffering and unadulterated evil, it is important for us to affirm that element of the Apostle's Creed, that "he shall come to judge the living and the dead."

There is more than God's judgment in the story; there is also God's grace. The narrative focuses on God and—in a bold move—describes God in terms of a hurting parent or a betrayed lover. "…the LORD was sorry that he had made humankind on the earth, and it grieved him to his heart."[122] As Walter Brueggemann puts it,

> God is not angered but grieved. He is not enraged but saddened. God does not stand over against but with his creation.[123]

And the story ends with grace. God makes a promise:

> I will never again curse the ground because of humankind, for the inclination of the human heart is evil from youth;

---

[121] David Brooks, "Harvey, Irma, Josey and Noah." *The New York Times* September 12, 2017, 27.
https://www.nytimes.com/2017/09/12/opinion/harvey-irma-jose-and-noah.html?smprod=nytcore-ipad&smid=nytcore-ipad-share
[122] Genesis 6:6.
[123] Walter Brueggemann *Genesis A Bible Commentary for Teaching and Preaching.* Louisville, KY: Westminster John Knox Press, 1982, 77.

> nor will I ever again destroy every living creature as I have done.[124]

Note: the human heart is still evil—nothing has changed. But God has changed: he will never again destroy every living creature. And one of the details of the story with an on-going resonance is the picture of the dove returning with a sprig of olive as indication that the flood has abated, and a new life is possible, even if humans have not changed.

It's therefore clear that the meaning of the biblical flood story is about God's grace, God's desire to persevere with humankind, despite our propensity for violence and rebellion and going our own way. And the grace is most clearly seen in the image of the dove with the sprig of olive in its mouth. It was an inspired move that made the olive branch a metaphor for peace, reconciliation and a new start.

And the dove imagery makes a second, telling appearance in scripture at the baptism of Jesus, where Jesus hears scripture affirming him as God's Son and calling him to the role of Isaiah's Suffering Servant, to suffer and die at the hands of sinful humanity. The dove represents the power of the Spirit, given to lead Jesus throughout his ministry and strengthen and sustain him to the end, and, according to Romans 1[125], being actively engaged in his resurrection.

So the promise of new life and the presence and power of the Spirit are acknowledged by the inclusion of the dove in the Presbyterian seal.

But the meaning of the dove comes powerfully into view in the words of Jesus in Matthew 10:16—

> Be wise as serpents and innocent as doves.

With these words, our Lord offers wisdom for Christians, to shape our response to the atrocities that continue to appall and bewilder

---

[124] Genesis 8:21.
[125] Romans 1:4 ... who was declared to be the Son of God with power according to the Spirit of holiness by resurrection from the dead.

us—both in this country and throughout the world. The President was right last week to call the Las Vegas shootings evil. The failure to uncover the shooter's motivation underscores the diagnosis. Evil is often irrational, inexplicable.

All last week the wisdom of the pundits of left and right has been on display and no doubt there will be congregations today who will hear sermons addressing the topic of continuing gun violence in our land. You don't want to hear my view on that—when episodes like Las Vegas occur, I share the shock every American feels, but the reactions those episodes produce remind me that I was not born here and start from different presuppositions. And so I feel a sermon is not the place to discuss guns, not only because you can't get a word in edgeways (!)—although I'm sure the topic will come up in today's Bible class after worship.

What's clear from all the talk this week is that there is no fail-safe solution to this problem. All the gun legislation we could imagine can't guarantee the eradication of this evil. But we are not powerless against it, if we take Jesus' words to heart: wise as serpents and gentle as doves.

If you think about the greatest evil our generation has encountered, most people would name communism—the cruelty and death inflicted in the name of that creed beggars the imagination.

Communism still survives in Cuba, China and North Korea, although none of them is fundamentally strong today, but otherwise, communism is finished. Over. Ronald Regan is credited with being a major catalyst in the downfall of the Soviet Union, and that represents the "wise as serpents" part of Jesus' words. In the face of evil, resistance is called for. And Regan's wise development of a credible deterrent made him, in the words of Jackie Kennedy's letter to Khrushchev, one of "the big men"[126] the world needs to fight evil.

---

[126] Jackie Kennedy's Letter to Khrushchev, December 1, 1963. She wrote, "The danger which troubled my husband was that war might be started not so much by the big men as by the little ones. While big men know the needs for self-control and restraint—little men are sometimes moved more by fear and pride." Her words continue to resonate today!   Accessed at
https://history.state.gov/historicaldocuments/frus1961-63v06/d120

Stories to Live By

But there's Jesus' other dimension, "gentle as doves." That's where Christians wield the weapon of prayer, especially prayer linked to the working of the Spirit in the world.

In his book on Prayer,[127] Philip Yancey tells the story of Laszlo Tokes, pastor of a small church of Hungarians living in communist Romania in the 1980s. He followed a pastor who had supported the communists to the point of wearing a red star on his clerical robes! Not Tokes. He denounced injustice, criticized the government and began to grow his church with Hungarian and Romanian dissidents. Membership grew from 40 persons to five thousand.

The authorities threatened him and then one night decided to evict him. Word spread and hundreds of Christians—Baptist, Orthodox, Reformed and Catholic alike—gathered and surrounded his house as a wall of protection. They stood night and day singing hymns and holding candles. After a few days, the police broke through and seized Tokes. The crowd then marched to the police station, growing when others heard what was going on, until it numbered 200,000.

Troops arrived and in one bloody incident fired on the crowd killing a hundred and wounding many more. A pastor came forward to try to prevent more violence. His first words were, "Let us pray," and Yancey recalls,

> In one spontaneous motion that giant mass of farmers, teachers, students, doctors and ordinary working people fell to their knees and recited the Lord's Prayer—a corporate act of civil disobedience. Within days the protest spread to the capital city of Bucharest, and a short time later that government that had ruled Romania with an iron fist toppled to the ground.[128]

Yancey followed that story with similar stories from Poland, East Germany and South Africa ... all demonstrating the difference prayer makes. He closes his chapter with words from Walter Wink:

---

[127] Philip Yancey, *Prayer Does It Make Any difference?* Grand Rapids, MI. Zondervan, 2006.
[128] Yancey, *Prayer, 119-1220.*

> The message is clear, history belongs to the intercessors, who believe the future into being.

… to which Yancey adds, "the pray-ers are essential agents in the final victory over evil suffering and death."[129]

There's the Spirt at work in the world, bringing God's grace to counter evil. Remember Paul's description of the difference the Spirit makes:

> the works of the flesh are obvious: fornication, impurity, licentiousness, idolatry, sorcery, enmities, strife, jealousy, anger, quarrels, dissensions, factions, envy, drunkenness, carousing, and things like these.

And, wow! are these prevailing characteristics of our culture today! By contrast

> … the fruit of the Spirit is love, joy, peace, patience, kindness, generosity, faithfulness, gentleness, and self-control.[130]

Evil will only be mastered by God's grace. We need a Christian response to current turmoil, we need the Spirit, we need to pray, much more than we do, for our nation and our leaders and for all the world.

Lord, take us and shake us, bless us and distress us until, by your Spirit's working in our lives, we are eager for your kingdom, impatient for its progress and willing to be people through whom your Spirit works to do your will and heal your world. In Jesus' name, Amen.

---

[129] Yancey, *Prayer* 130, citing Walter Wink, *Engaging the Powers*, Philadelphia Fortress Press, 1992, 229.
[130] Galatians 5:19-22.

The Trouble with Nature

The Sunday after hurricane Irma

Psalm 29

Ascribe to the LORD, O heavenly beings,
  ascribe to the LORD glory and strength.
Ascribe to the LORD the glory of his name;
  worship the LORD in holy splendor.

The voice of the LORD is over the waters;
  the God of glory thunders,
  the LORD, over mighty waters.
The voice of the LORD is powerful;
  the voice of the LORD is full of majesty.

The voice of the LORD breaks the cedars;
  the LORD breaks the cedars of Lebanon.
He makes Lebanon skip like a calf,
  and Sirion like a young wild ox.

The voice of the LORD flashes forth flames of fire.
The voice of the LORD shakes the wilderness;
  the LORD shakes the wilderness of Kadesh.

The voice of the LORD causes the oaks to whirl,
  and strips the forest bare;
  and in his temple all say, 'Glory!'

The LORD sits enthroned over the flood;
  the LORD sits enthroned as king for ever.
May the LORD give strength to his people!
  May the LORD bless his people with peace.

It's good to be in church after hurricane Irma, and share relief that the storm has passed. We can be grateful that although people lost their lives in the storm, we did not. We can feel for those who suffered damage, especially when the damage amounted to total destruction of home and the loss of all possessions. We can be grateful of all the support that the storm called forth, and the willingness of so many to go the second mile—and the third and the fourth …

And if you're thinking, now that the storm has passed life can get back to normal, let me offer a word of caution: Don't. Don't move on without taking on board the lessons of Irma, because I believe we can learn from the lessons of the past week in ways that can strengthen our faith. So don't forget Irma.

Don't forget what Irma revealed about our vulnerability. In Florida, we do live in a paradise of sorts, surrounded by natural beauty and bathed in seemingly perpetual sunshine, with just a bit of humidity thrown in to dampen our superlatives. Fine, but Irma reminded us that there's another side to nature—storms which, for all our science, we cannot fully predict and which, for all our technology, we cannot control.

And perhaps that's one of the most important lessons to ponder. We sometimes rattle around the world thinking we're in charge, that it's all up to us and we can do whatever comes into our minds to do.

We sometimes assume that our sophistication, or our wealth, or some other asset can bring security, and Irma debunked that assumption. Billionaire tycoon Sir Richard Branson was no more able to defend his Caribbean home on Necker Island from Irma that the poorest family living on nearby Barbuda.

We forget that we are tenants, not owners of the world, dependents, not creators.

A bit of humility as a response to our vulnerability would do us good.

That's what makes Psalm 29 such an appropriate scripture, showing that we can find in scripture a word of guidance and help for almost any situation we encounter. Who said the Bible's out of date? Psalm 29 is a hymn of praise inspired by the awesome power of nature. The psalmist witnessed a powerful thunderstorm sweeping in from the Mediterranean, through Lebanon and down to the southern desert

(vv. 7-8). The storm reminds him of powers in nature capable of overwhelming human life.

His thinking moves from one storm to the power of nature overall to overwhelm human life. He realizes how precarious human life can be before the force of nature.

In face of such thoughts, the psalmist affirms his faith: that God is greater than the forces of nature. God is greater than the destruction of the storm and its threat to life. And his sense of awe at the power of nature drives him to prayer, with which the psalm ends:

> May the LORD give strength to his people!
> May the LORD bless his people with peace! (v.11)

Vulnerable before the forces of nature, he seeks God's help and he prays for faith. A good response to Irma's lessons.

Not everyone learns that lesson, sadly, so secondly, don't forget what Irma revealed about human nature.

It's amazing the way a crisis reveals a person's true colors and the colors did not always make for a pretty picture.

- There were the looters, of course, there always are: people who place self-enrichment above self-respect, and who value money more than morality. Fear of looting made some people refuse to evacuate, placing their own and others' lives at risk.
- Then there were the idiots: posting dramatic hoax photos and videos of fake sharks and past tsunamis, intending no doubt to aggravate the legitimate fears that people harbored.
- Then there were the people Piers Morgan described as "the selfie-loving clowns"

> … who think a hurricane is a great chance to film themselves surfing, or tying their bodies to a tree, or walking out over areas where the sea had withdrawn, oblivious to

the fact that they inevitably steal rescuers' attention away from those who didn't deliberately court their difficulties.[131]

Happily, there's another side.

- There are the first responders who work long and perilous shifts to rescue, help or preserve.
- There are the volunteers who use their boats to navigate floods to help people to safety.
- There was the Houston pastor who swam in flood waters for hours, checking submerged cars in case there was someone trapped inside.
- And those nature lovers who cared for the manatees stranded when Irma's winds drove the waters out of the gulf
- And the neighborliness that breaks out when homes are opened to evacuees, and, after the storm, when felled trees have to be removed, and food carried to homes without power … and so on.

Such manifestations of our common humanity are heartwarming and heartbreaking. Heartwarming because they show a quality of mercy that enriches life. Heartbreaking because we rarely see it practiced, far less celebrated in our culture.

When help was offered, rescue activated, no one asked, "Whom did you vote for as President?" "What do you think about Obamacare?" or even "Who should get the biggest tax cuts?"

Deeper than our divisions, higher than our hang-ups, more powerful than our politics was our better human nature. If only that were normal! Why can't we learn the lesson of Irma—why, indeed, does it need a hurricane to show us there is a better way to live than our tribal bitterness and our isolationist selfishness. Jesus called it 'loving your neighbor as yourself.' Unless we learn this lesson, we are doomed.

---

[131] Piers Morgan "How Harvey and Irma Brought out the Best in America, finally made the President presidential and reminded CNN What it should be doing." Mail Online, dailymail.co.uk September 11, 2017.

And the lessons Irma brought range wider than our shores. Parts of our country have been badly hit. Parts of the Caribbean much worse. Mexico has hurricane and earthquake. In Asia monsoon-season flooding is at an all-time high and thousands perish.

Meanwhile, we need (or so we think) to spend millions more on armaments, and to keep us entertained, millions are spent on sporting stars, and millions more are spent by Hollywood to produce what *The Wall Street Journal* last month dubbed "This Summer of Duds."[132]

Meanwhile, western countries find that budgets for foreign aid must be cut and help denied to the most helpless people on the planet. Isn't it remarkable that it takes successful businessmen like Warren Buffet and Bill Gates to be the conscience of the west and be strong advocates for the strong helping the weak? The report issued last week by the Gates Foundation spoke of the danger of losing the progress that has been achieved in 18 Sustainable Growth Developments such as reducing infant mortality, HIV deaths, improving health care, sanitation etc.[133]

Earlier this year at the TED 2017 conference on power, interaction and the future in Vancouver, Pope Francis teleconferenced a TED Talk in which he called for a "revolution of tenderness." Some snippets:

> We all need each other, none of us is an island, an autonomous and independent 'I,' separated from the other and we can only build the future by standing together, including everyone.
>
> How wonderful would it be if the growth of scientific and technological innovation would come along with more equality and social inclusion. How wonderful would it be,

---

[132] Erich Schwartzel "Movie Theaters Have a Bigger Problem Than This Summer of Duds" *The Wall Street Journal*, August 11, 2017.
[133] Bill and Melinda Gates "Goal Keepers, the Stories Behind the Data." http://www.globalgoals.org/goalkeepers/datareport/

while we discover faraway planets, to rediscover the needs of the brothers and sisters orbiting around us.[134]

Don't forget what Irma revealed about our world. The trouble with nature is that it is troubled—both in the natural world and the human heart.

The meaning of Christ's great commandment carries important implications. Included in the command to love the Lord our God must be the requirement that we tread gently in God's world and take a more responsible attitude towards nature. We can no longer ignore the challenge of climate change and the likelihood that future storms and other natural disasters will increase in frequency and severity. The concern of the business community that addressing climate change will cause costs to increase should be offset by the awareness that hurricanes don't come cheap, nor floods nor fires.

It's time to acknowledge the truth of the words we sing:

> *God made the world and at its birth ordained our human race*
> *To live as stewards of the earth, responding to God's grace.*
> *But we are vain and sadly proud, we sow not peace but strife*
> *Our discord spreads a deadly cloud that threatens all of life.*[135]

The command that that we love our neighbor requires that we do something to make the world a better place and show our lively gratitude for faith and its assurance of God's love. The spontaneous generosity, patient comforting, sometimes heroic rescuing should be fostered and celebrated, not located behind some glass case and labeled "For Emergency Use Only."

May the LORD give strength to his people!
  May the LORD bless his people with peace.

---

[134] https://www.ted.com/talks/pope_francis_why_the_only_future_worth_building_includes_everyone/transcript
[135] H Kenn Carmichael, "Today We All Are Called to Be Disciples" in *the Presbyterian Hymnal* Louisville, KY> Westminster John Knox Press, 1990 #434.

Beyond the Harold Meeker Syndrome
1 Cor 12:12-31a

For just as the body is one and has many members, and all the members of the body, though many, are one body, so it is with Christ. For in the one Spirit we were all baptized into one body—Jews or Greeks, slaves or free—and we were all made to drink of one Spirit. Indeed, the body does not consist of one member but of many. If the foot would say, "Because I am not a hand, I do not belong to the body," that would not make it any less a part of the body. And if the ear would say, "Because I am not an eye, I do not belong to the body," that would not make it any less a part of the body. If the whole body were an eye, where would the hearing be? If the whole body were hearing, where would the sense of smell be? But as it is, God arranged the members in the body, each one of them, as he chose. If all were a single member, where would the body be? As it is, there are many members, yet one body. The eye cannot say to the hand, "I have no need of you," nor again the head to the feet, "I have no need of you." On the contrary, the members of the body that seem to be weaker are indispensable, and those members of the body that we think less honorable we clothe with greater honor, and our less respectable members are treated with greater respect; whereas our more respectable members do not need this. But God has so arranged the body, giving the greater honor to the inferior member, that there may be no dissension within the body, but the members may have the same care for one another. If one member suffers, all suffer together with it; if one member is honored, all rejoice together with it.

Now you are the body of Christ and individually members of it. And God has appointed in the church first apostles, second prophets, third teachers; then deeds of power, then gifts of healing, forms of assistance, forms of leadership, various kinds of tongues. Are all apostles? Are all prophets? Are all teachers? Do all work miracles? Do all possess gifts of healing? Do all speak in tongues? Do all interpret? But strive for the greater gifts. And I will show you a still more excellent way

1 Cor 12:27 Now you are the body of Christ and individually members of it.

Norman M. Pritchard

I think Gary Larson is a great cartoonist. His series, *The Far Side*, offers subtle, provocative and subversive takes on the way things are and the way we sometimes are. Many of his characters are animals who speak and act exactly the way humans do, but shouldn't.

One cartoon shows a television news program covering an airline disaster. In the background there is the chaos of the downed aircraft and the disorder of the emergency vehicles—there's noise and confusion everywhere. The reporter covering the story is a bird—and I mean a creature with wings and feathers: I'm not being rude at the expense of female journalists!

It's a horrible disaster, with major loss of life. And the reporter is saying,

> ... we understand that the name of the bird sucked into the jet's engine was Harold Meeker.

Pointed, isn't it? Ignore the size of the disaster; and the question of survivors: the important thing on birds' TV is the bird involved, whose name was Harold Meeker.

Larson has shown up a human failing which is universal. We have TV channels who boast that they are the channel "Where local news comes first" because, let's face it, that's what we're interested in—us and the people just like us.

The ancient Greeks called this failing myopia—mouse eyes; but I think it's better named the Harold Meeker Syndrome. It's everywhere.

When I was growing up in Glasgow, major national or international news stories would spill over into BBC Scotland; and their news would begin, "Scottish reaction to ... the Budget ... the General Election ... the arms deal ..." or whatever. And if there's an Australian caught up in a hostage drama in one of the world's trouble spots, you can be sure that that's the angle which the TV news in Melbourne or in Sydney plays. Us and people just like us—the Harold Meeker Syndrome.

It's not restricted to the TV news. Whatever stratum of society we occupy, entry is guaranteed to someone who is "One of us." To brand a person "One of them" is to encourage exclusion, discrimination or, in trouble spots like the Middle East or Myanmar, something infinitely worse.

You even find it in the church. Donald McGavran started "The Church Growth Movement" on this basis. He called it the 'homogeneous unit principle' but it was really the Harold Meeker Syndrome in religious disguise. McGavran argued that churches grow better when they're homogeneous units, that is, made up of people "just like us." It's so much more comfortable that way. Everyone's alike, so there are no surprises, no awkward dissonance. Everyone agrees, so there are no disputes. According to McGavran's principle, the church grows best when it is a cozy fellowship of people "just like us."

I actually once heard a Church Growth exponent tell a story of a church down south which split during the civil rights era over the issue of race. It became two churches, one segregated, one integrated, and they set up in competition on opposite sides of the main street in town. Over the years, they both grew to the same size as the old undivided church had been. 100% church growth, he enthused. Isn't that wonderful? Well, only if the gospel doesn't matter; only if numbers are more important than Christ's love. And that's the trouble with the Christian version of the Harold Meeker Syndrome: it seeks to fill the church with cookie-cutter Christians, all alike. There's no stretching of our horizons; no challenge to our thinking, no stimulus to grow and reach for deeper understandings and more enriching relationships.

And God designs the body of Christ to overcome that weakness. Jesus calls 12 disciples, none of them alike, all of them necessary for his gospel ministry. After Easter, his followers write the story down. Matthew tells of Jesus the new Moses, the teacher, the rabbi of Israel, the fulfillment of scripture—locating him in the history and expectation of Israel. Luke, the outsider, tells a different story—or, rather, the same story in a different way: he notices outsiders, the women Matthew rarely noticed, and shepherds, lepers, Samaritans, Gentiles. Who is right? Both are. Which Gospel could you do without? Neither. You can apply the same questions to Mark and John and get the same result; both are different, and both are needed.

Same with us. God engrafts us into the body of Christ to overcome the Harold Meeker weakness: to give us a place where we may contribute our understanding and experience, our gifts and opportunities, and where others' similar contributions may deepen and expand ours, so that together we paint a bigger picture on a wider canvas.

And God's love is big enough to embrace all of us and all our differences. The diversity of the church becomes our affirmation of the greatness of God's love and the richness of his grace. Ephesians talks about the boundless, unsearchable, riches of Christ: they're so deep and wide that most of us only ever catch a glimpse of one or other aspect of their power and scope.

And so God gives us in the church Billy Graham and John Shelby Spong, Annie Lamott and Marva Dawn, Tim La Haye and Martin Marty, Pope John Paul II and Hans Küng, and so on— complementary, sometimes almost contradictory Christians, each of them making their contribution and, through their contribution, challenging us to see beyond our own horizons, calling us to face a bigger God, to reach for deeper truth and strive for wider ministry and service.

George MacLeod[136] was right: "A great mystery is your church."

The diversity of the church may be sometimes uncomfortable, but it's essential. "You are the body of Christ," Paul writes, "and individually members of it." (v.27) And he reminds his readers what bodies are: hands, feet, eyes, ears; even what he delicately refers to as "those members of the body that we think less honorable." (Monty Python used to call them "the naughty parts"!) So many bits and pieces—and they're all needed!

---

[136] George MacLeod, *The Whole Earth Shall Cry Glory*. Iona: Wild Goose Publications, 1985, 37.

And they're needed because, as he says, "If the whole body were an eye, where would the hearing be...?" Paul points out that diversity is not just the way it happens to be, but also the way it has to be—indeed the way God wants it to be: "God has so arranged the body, ..." in this way, he says. God creates the diversity. This is the Lord's doing, and if we were alert to its meaning, it would be marvelous in our eyes.

Why marvelous? Well, because none of us are truly alike: we are each a unique amalgam of heredity and environment, tastes and training, abilities and experience, aptitudes and tastes. And that's fine; but few of us are willing to move beyond that range. And that is not so good.

When Aleksandr Solzhenitsyn was awarded the Nobel Prize for literature, his acceptance speech spoke about the "characteristic weakness" of the human race, "[our] ability to learn only from our own experience, so that the experience of others passes [us] by."[137]

Sometimes it's the experience of others that helps us grow.

Charles Campbell, who teaches at Columbia Seminary in Georgia, recalls a bad week from his pastorate days. The lectionary pointed him to praise as the theme for Sunday's sermon, and his week was filled with non-praise: heavy counseling in a bitter marriage breakdown; a runaway teenager, death and terminal illness.

He obviously ministered in a needy community: The Salvation Army sent people to his church—and things must be pretty bad when the Salvation Army makes referrals to the Presbyterians! His third referral that week was just too much. A seventy-year-old man, his sixty-five-year-old sister and her thirty-four-year-old severely disabled daughter were hitch-hiking from Kentucky to Louisiana. Their trailer-home had burned to the ground; they had lost everything. A Good Samaritan had driven them into town but was too distraught to help them further.

Campbell organized motel accommodation by phone and arranged to meet them Saturday morning to get some clothes and bus tickets for the journey. Remember he's working on a sermon he's supposed to preach on praise. In the morning, he recalls,

---

[137] Aleksandr Solzhenitsyn, *One Word of Truth*. London: Bodley Head, 1972,

> When I saw them, I was immediately depressed. But a few moments with them spoke good news to me, judged and healed me and confirmed the appropriateness of praise even this week. ... These people had praise in their hearts—despite everything that had happened to them. They were as kind and thoughtful as any people I'd ever met. They wanted very few clothes—but what they took was remarkable. The older woman chose the brightest orange blouse on the rack. And the daughter chose a pair of blindingly yellow slacks and a matching top. And they took some big old tennis shoes—soft and comfortable for the trip.
>
> That's all they took. That's all they wanted. As they were going out the door, they stopped and asked that we pray together. Before I could open my mouth, *they* did the praying! They praised God and gave thanks for the kindness people had shown on their journey, for the certainty of God's presence, for the upcoming arrival at their sister's house. Who could have imagined it? They were tired and sad. But at the same time, they were joyful in a strange and humble way ...[138]

Who indeed could have imagined it? I'll tell you who—people who know that the body of Christ is not just eyes and hands and ears and feet, but rather the eyes *of Christ* and the hands *of Christ* and the ears *of Christ* and the feet *of Christ*, because, it being his body, Christ is present and in the midst of it—owning it and acknowledging it and shaping it and directing it.

So, for example, in this part of the body of Christ, an experience like that from another part of the body of Christ might encourage us to hold on to the belief that God is present in the midst of trouble, strengthening and upholding his people. Then in our time of trouble we might trust that God is present, present even there.

Or we might catch an echo of the Master's words, "inasmuch as you have done it to one of the least of these my brothers and sisters ..."

---

[138] Charles L. Campbell, "Learning to Blush" in *Journal for Preachers* XXIV.4, Pentecost 2001, 49f.

and be encouraged again to take up what might have been discouraging ministry with hopeless cases.

Or we might be reminded of those who, as the church—and therefore in your name and mine and Christ's—minister in the tough places and the broken environments, seeking to incarnate the love of God. That might spur us to support or inspire us to play our part in some opportunity we can see.

Or we might find some other aspect resonating in some different way. Whatever: the experience of others—the role of hands, or eyes, or feet—encourage us to grow a deeper faith, attempt a wider ministry, trust a bigger God, who calls us all to be Christ's body, working in a broken and a needy world.

Light in the Darkness
Isaiah 9:2-4

A Meditation for a Longest Night service

The people who walked in darkness have seen a great light; those who lived in a land of deep darkness— on them light has shined. You have multiplied the nation, you have increased its joy; they rejoice before you as with joy at the harvest, as people exult when dividing plunder. For the yoke of their burden, and the bar across their shoulders, the rod of their oppressor, you have broken as on the day of Midian.

For those whose hearts are heavy in this season, things wouldn't be so difficult if only we didn't glaze over the Christmas story with sentimentality.

The Christmas story is a story of joy and gladness, to be sure, but there is much more to it than that. We have glossed over parts of the story that might particularly point us in the direction of help and hope.

There are lots of pain in the Christmas story. Some of it is personal.

Think of Mary's conception and the impact it must have had. Remember the loneliness of Joseph's decision, and what a huge thing it was that Joseph accepted Mary and stood by her. Think of the cruel gossip and loss of respect, and possibly loss of business for his pains.

Think of the birth in the stable, because there was no room in the inn. "The inn" is not right: there was no Bethlehem Hilton in those days. What is referred to was probably a guest chamber in a private home. And since Bethlehem was Joseph's ancestral home, he would have had family there, but no one in the wider family took the family in and offered hospitality. So add to the drama of childbirth, the awful surroundings, the abandonment and isolation. It was a long, dark night.

Then Matthew tells us of Herod's attempt to eliminate a potential rival to his throne—even though it would have been at least 20 years before any rival would have been ready for a challenge. The slaughter of the children in Bethlehem two years of age and under was the kind of callous, cruel, senseless violence that fills the headlines and speaks of the abuse of power in our day. Then, to escape that, the family fled to Egypt and the oh-so-current experience of refugee status.

That was the world Jesus entered, the reality Christ came to; Jesus assumed humanity exposed to all of that—vulnerable, open to pain and loss, lonely and afraid—and in it he offered the assurance of Emmanuel, God is with us, even in the midst of our pain.

The challenge of our pain is two-fold.

First to acknowledge it: to see that it is right to grieve the loss of a loved one, the ending of a dream, the shattering of a hope which turns our lives upside down. Our culture is keen to move us on from the bad experiences and seek closure, usually far too quickly. Pain is important as an affirmation of the value of what we have lost.

Remember the days before digital photographs. You took your roll of film to the store and with your prints you also got the negatives. And they *were* negative: everything was the wrong way around: light colors were dark and dark colors light. Pain works like that: it is the negative impression of the positive that has been lost, and as such is an expression of the value of what has been lost. Scripture gives us permission to grieve our losses and lament them. Laments are the second most common poems in the book of Psalms—one third of the total content of the book.

But grieve within limits. The more grievous the loss, the greater the danger that we allow it to spill over other areas of our lives and conceal the other good things that have not been lost. It takes deliberate choice not to let that happen: to notice, affirm and hold onto the blessings that have not been taken away.

Alyce Mackenzie writes interestingly about the birth of her brother, years ago, back in the days when mothers-to-be shared a hospital room, divided by a curtain. Her brother arrived hale and hearty, but the baby born to the lady in the next bed was stillborn. Mackenzie says,

> My mother woke up the next morning and could see her roommate standing at the window, her face in profile looking out. She was whispering over and over again words from Psalm 118:12, "This is the day the Lord has made. I will rejoice and be glad in it. This is the day that the Lord has made. I will rejoice and be glad in it."
>
> "How can you say that today of all days?" my mother couldn't help but ask.
>
> "Why should today be unlike any other day?" the woman replied.[139]

Loss, yes; pain and sadness, of course; but more than that. There was still the love and mercy of God and blessings to be seen and tasted and affirmed alongside the pain. And affirming the blessings is like touching the hem of Christ's garment: his healing power begins to flow and slowly we reach for the belief that we can get through this, by God's grace.

Emmanuel, God with us. perhaps most especially with us in the darkness and pain.

> The people who walked in darkness have seen a great light, The light shines in the darkness, and the darkness did not overcome it.

May it be so for you, this Christmas.

---

[139] http://www.patheos.com//Progressive-Christian/Any-News-Alyce-McKenzie-12-16-2013.html?utm_source=feedburner&utm_medium=email&utm_campaign=Feed%3A+patheos%2FNzEA+%28Column+-+Edgy+Exegesis%29

It *Is* About Me!

A Meditation for Christmas Eve, 2004

I hope you all have a very merry, joyful and blessed Christmas!

Fortunately, we're in church and I can make that statement safely. Outside, that wish would be regarded as somewhere between politically incorrect and downright offensive. It's become our latest national tradition that the weeks leading up to Christmas are filled with complaints about religion escaping from places of worship and intruding into the public domain.

There's been plenty of evidence of this recently:

- In different parts of the country schools have again banned Christmas carols, even orchestral versions that have no words.

- One New Jersey school district even banned "Rudolph the Red-Nosed Reindeer" from a concert, because it mentions Christmas Eve.

- The mayor of Somerville, Mass., apologized for mistakenly calling his December celebration a "Christmas party." He said he should have called it a "holiday party."[140]

(Ha! wait till he finds out that 'holiday' was originally 'holy day.'!!)

An article in today's *Wall Street Journal* points out:

> Many believe the father of [the concept of] the department store is R.H. Macy, and how ironic it is that Macy's namesake store on [New York's] Herald Square is no longer famous for "The Miracle on 34th Street" but for banning "Christmas" from its premises.

---

[140] Data from two articles: James Q Wilson, "Christmas and Christianity", and Katherine Kersten, "Bring Back Those Silver Bells." *The Wall Street Journal*, Friday, December 24, 2004, Internet Edition.

> [And, of course] Target department stores ... told the Salvation Army's Christmas kettle ringers there was no room for them within range of the stores' front doors...[141]

So while the Christmas carol proclaims, "'Tis the season to be jolly," there are many people who would prefer "'Tis the season to be grumpy!" Add to the mix ...

- the number of movies that have a distinct anti-Christmas mood,
- the growing number of 'I hate Christmas' web sites, now running into thousands.
- and books like *I Hate Christmas—303 Reasons Why You Should Too,*[142]

... and you're left with the feeling that there's something wrong if you want to celebrate and have a merry Christmas.

You know, of course, the problem: the celebration of the holy day has become too self-serving. Too many people think, It's all about me.

Did you see the newspaper advertisements being run by a major publishing house, with several best-sellers on show, under the slogan, "Read Them Before You Wrap Them (no one will ever know.)"[143] It's all about me.

In early December, I received an e-mail from Amazon.com, which said,

> Just because we make gift shopping so easy doesn't mean you shouldn't reward yourself for all the cheer you've

---

[141] Daniel Henninger, "Whence Came The U.S. Tradition To Give and Give?" in *The Wall Street Journal*, Friday, December 24, 2004, Internet Edition
[142] There are several books with this title, which confirms my point!
[143] Advert for Time Warner Books, *New York Times Book Review*, Sunday December 5, 2004, 44-45.

spread. Take a look at these items we recommend for you and just tell yourself: you've earned it.[144]

We've got to be the ones being served—even when we're giving gifts. It's all about me.

A letter in last Sunday's *New York Times* is my favorite. The author wrote—and I promise you, I'm not making this up—

> ... For years, I have been ridiculed and maligned for buying my own Christmas presents in a wide price range and selling them to anyone who wishes to give me presents.
>
> This reasonable approach gets me exactly what I want and saves the gift giver from having to shop. And we both avoid that awkward moment of exchanging gifts and reassurances about said gifts.
>
> Any unsold gifts are either returned, put away until ...my birthday ... or used anyway.[145]

He really thinks it's all about him!! The poor guy doesn't understand that what's important in gifts is not what you get; but *why you get it*. The gift is the expression of something bigger—the relationship between the giver and the receiver.

Now this may be the moment when you are expecting a Christian pastor to launch into an attack on the values of our culture. You know: you expect a pastor to ask, Are we so self-serving, so self-obsessed, that everything becomes an excuse for our gratification ... Shouldn't there be some time when someone gets to say, "It isn't about you"?

And, to be sure, such a pastor would have a point. Some of the Christmas happenings are offensive. But while I too regret the materialism and the self-serving, I want to be allowed a second thought.

---

[144] E-mail from Amazon.com
[145] Sky Cole, "That Present 'Neath The Tree I Bought for Me" in *The New York Times*, Letters Page, Sunday December 19, 2004, WK 10.

Norman M. Pritchard

Because it strikes me that, below the surface, there is something deeper, trying to find expression and get out.

- Our compulsive need for things may arise from a deeper need—for fulfillment; because many people are leading lives which have no meaning.

- Our panic to get gift-giving right points to a longing for healthy and satisfying relationships in our lives.

- All our careful planning to get everything right is driven by a wish for joy in our lives that lasts and is simple and real.

- Perhaps even the need to exclude things religious from the public domain is a fear that values and ambitions might be called in question by a probing spirituality that points us to our neighbor for sake of the Christ who laid his glory by for us.

And if that's the case, then many of the excesses I've mentioned are perhaps only distorted versions of what Christmas is all about.

It *is* about me: because it was for me that Jesus came into the world! It was for you that Jesus came into the world —for each one of us— that Jesus came, to seek and to help and to save.

When the shepherds in the Christmas story hear of the birth of the Savior, they are told,

> …. to you is born this day in the city of David, a Savior, the Messiah, the Lord.

It is about you; and the birth of Jesus represents tidings of great joy for all the people.

Because in the Baby of Bethlehem, God has come to earth, in love, for you.

- Offering in Christ, life more abundant; a way to live that brings fulfillment and enrichment day by day.

- Bringing the love which Christ lived, and letting it loose in people's hearts: love that...

  ...is patient and kind ...does not seek its own way... it bears all things, believes all things, hopes all things endures all things – love never ends!

- Offering, in Christ, forgiveness for the past and hope for the future which bring joy that nothing else on earth can touch.

It is about me, it is about you because God loves us and has sent us Jesus.

> ...to you is born this day in the city of David, a Savior who is the Messiah, the Lord.

Appendix

General Assembly Guidelines for the use of Scripture in the church

1 Recognize that Jesus Christ, the Redeemer, is the center of scripture.

2 Let the focus be on the plain text of scripture, on the grammatical and historical context, rather than on allegory and subjective fantasy.

3 Depend upon the guidance of the Holy Spirit in interpreting and applying God's message.

4 Be guided by the doctrinal consensus of the church, which is the rule of faith.

5 Let all interpretations be in accord with the rule of love, the two-fold commandment to love God and to love our neighbor.

6 Remember that interpretation of the Bible requires earnest study in order to establish the best text and to interpret the influence of the historical and cultural context in which the divine message has come.

7 Seek to interpret a particular passage of the Bible in light of the whole Bible

Approved by the General Assembly of the United Presbyterian Church (USA) 1982; reprinted by permission from *Selected Theological Statements of the Presbyterian Church (USA) General Assemblies 1956-1998*, Christian Faith and Life, Congregational Ministries Division, Presbyterian Church (USA).

www.ingramcontent.com/pod-product-compliance
Lightning Source LLC
Chambersburg PA
CBHW071913110526
44591CB00011B/1668